# Vorschläge für Klassenarbeiten

## Vorwort

Die übergreifende Zielsetzung des modernen Englischunterrichts ist es, die Lernenden zur Kommunikation in der Zielsprache zu befähigen. Sie sollen in die Lage versetzt werden, in konkreten Situationen sprachlich adäquat zu handeln. Im Vordergrund des Unterrichts bzw. von *Password Orange 6 Erweiterungskurs* stehen Themen und Situationen, die an die Erfahrungen Heranwachsender anknüpfen und auch eine interkulturelle Betrachtung ermöglichen. Damit die Schülerinnen und Schüler situationsgerecht sprachlich handeln können, erwerben sie die notwendigen sprachlichen Mittel (Wortschatz, Redemittel, Grammatik); sie lernen, mit verschiedenen Hör- und Lesetexten umzugehen und eigene Texte zunehmend selbstständig zu erstellen. Darüber hinaus werden ihnen Techniken vermittelt, die ihnen helfen, ihre Lern- und Arbeitsprozesse effektiver zu organisieren.

Die Klassenarbeiten decken folgende Erwartungen ab:
- interkulturelles Wissen,
- die Kenntnis sprachlicher Mittel und die Fähigkeit, diese beim Verstehen und Verfassen von Texten anzuwenden,
- die Fähigkeit, Lern- und Arbeitsprozesse zu gestalten.

In den hier vorgeschlagenen schriftlichen Aufgaben und/oder Klassenarbeiten sollen die Lernenden die erworbenen Fähigkeiten, Fertigkeiten und Kenntnisse in sinnvollen Sprachverwendungszusammenhängen nachweisen.
Alle relevanten Bereiche und Teilbereiche sollten annähernd gleichgewichtig in den Klassenarbeiten eines Schuljahres berücksichtigt werden. Deshalb empfiehlt es sich, die Klassenarbeiten zu Beginn eines Schuljahres in die didaktische Planung einzubeziehen.

### Zur Konzeption der Aufgaben und Klassenarbeiten für *Password Orange 6 Erweiterungskurs*

Wie aus den Übersichten, die den Aufgabenkatalogen jeweils vorangestellt sind, hervorgeht, sind zu jeder *Topic* des Schülerbuchs vier bzw. fünf Aufgaben entwickelt worden. Jede Aufgabe besteht aus mehreren aufeinander bezogenen Teilaufgaben. Ausgangspunkt der Aufgaben sind verschiedene Textsorten, HV-Texte und Bildergeschichten mit Auswertungen. Jeweils die ersten ein bis zwei Aufgaben dienen der Textsicherung. Weitere Aufgaben erwarten von S komplexe Sprachleistungen. Der Lehrperson bietet sich mit den unterschiedlichen Aufgabenstellungen die Möglichkeit, die Klassenarbeit nach dem Baukastenprinzip für die Lerngruppe individuell nach Lerntempo und Lernleistung der S zusammenzustellen. In der Regel sollten zwei bis drei Aufgaben genügen, um die Sprachkompetenz der S zu überprüfen, vor allem dann, wenn ein Text als Ausgangspunkt der Aufgabe gewählt wird. Eine von S am Ende der Klassenarbeit überprüfte und korrigierte Endfassung der Sprachprodukte erscheint sinnvoller als die Lösung vieler einzelner Teilaufgaben.

Bei den Transferaufgaben könnte es sich auch anbieten, S eine Wahlmöglichkeit zu geben.
Die HV-Aufgaben bieten neben der Überprüfung des globalen und des Detailverständnisses auch eine Ausweitung, in der der Hörtext Grundlage einer inhaltlichen Auseinandersetzung mit dem Gehörten ist (*argumentation, creative writing, etc.*).
Die Aufgaben und Klassenarbeiten beziehen sich vor allem auf die Lernschwerpunkte der jeweiligen *Topic* (vgl. Übersichten). Die Lernschwerpunkte werden folgenden Bereichen zugeordnet: **Wo:** Wortschatz, **Gr:** Grammatik, **T:** Textform, **LV:** Leseverstehen, **HV:** Hörverstehen, **LA:** Lern- und Arbeitstechniken und **Wi:** Wissen.

Alle Aufgaben sind als **Kopiervorlagen** konzipiert. Diese umfassen die Aufgabenstellung/Arbeitsanweisung, ggf. ein Beispiel.
In Form und Anlage orientieren sich die Aufgaben an den im Unterricht mit *Password Orange 6 Erweiterungskurs* praktizierten Vermittlungsverfahren und Einübungssituationen, so dass auch die Lernerfolgsüberprüfung weitgehend integriert und in situativer Einbettung geschieht: Den Aufgaben liegt immer eine konkrete, in der Einleitung oder Arbeitsanweisung beschriebene Kommunikationssituation zugrunde. Diese wird in den meisten Fällen präzisiert, indem einige der wichtigen konstitutiven Elemente wie Ort und Zeit, die handelnden Personen, die Mitteilungsabsicht und die damit verbundene Textform genannt werden.
Da zu jeder *Topic* mehrere umfangreiche Klassenarbeitsvorschläge vorliegen, empfiehlt es sich, eines der drei Angebote als Übungsmaterial wahrzunehmen. Teile der Angebote können als Vorübung im Unterricht oder als schriftliche Übung verwendet werden. S gewöhnen sich so leichter an die Anforderungen der eigentlichen Klassenarbeit.

Die Aufgaben sind so konzipiert, dass S ihre Kenntnisse, Fertigkeiten und Fähigkeiten, Texte zu verstehen und zu verfassen, nachweisen können. Die Aufgabentypen sind deshalb überwiegend halboffen oder offen.

**Geschlossene Aufgaben** sind inhaltlich und sprachlich so konstruiert, dass sie in der Regel nur eine Lösungsmöglichkeit zulassen. Die Lernenden erbringen eine punktuelle Leistung; die Ergebnisse sind vorhersagbar.

**Halboffene Aufgaben** sind weniger gelenkt. Der Entscheidungsspielraum der Lernenden und ihre Ausdrucksmöglichkeiten sind größer als bei geschlossenen Aufgaben. Die sprachlichen Ergebnisse sind nicht mehr genau vorhersagbar. In den halboffenen Aufgaben werden den Lernenden Hilfen unterschiedlicher Art gegeben.

Die Hilfen können sich auf Sprache, Inhalt oder Arbeitstechniken beziehen. Sie sind:
- sprachlicher Art, indem z. B. auf Strukturen hingewiesen wird, die zu verwenden sind,

## Vorschläge für Klassenarbeiten

- inhaltlicher Art, indem z. B. die zu behandelnden Aspekte genannt werden,
- arbeitstechnischer Art, indem z. B. eine Anleitung zur Ideen- oder Informationserfassung (z. B. *grid*) mitgegeben oder der erwartete Umfang (Anzahl der Sätze) des Textes festgesetzt wird.

**Offene Aufgaben** eröffnen den Lernenden einen größeren gestalterischen Spielraum. Es werden komplexe Leistungen auf der sprachlichen und inhaltlichen Ebene verlangt. Diese Aufgaben enthalten dementsprechend weniger Lenkung und Hilfen.

In schriftlichen Arbeiten der Klasse 10 sollten geschlossene Aufgaben, die den Lernenden keine Freiräume in Bezug auf Inhalt und Sprache gewähren, auf wenige Aufgaben beschränkt sein, z. B. zur Überprüfung von Verstehensleistungen und Grammatik- und Wortschatzkenntnissen. In jeder Klassenarbeit in der Jahrgangsstufe 10 müssen die S zusammenhängende Texte erstellen. Es empfiehlt sich daher, sie mit einem zweisprachigen Wörterbuch arbeiten zu lassen. Das dürfte keine Schwierigkeiten bereiten, da S auf den Umgang mit dem Wörterbuch durch die *Strategy pages* in *Password Orange 6 Erweiterungskurs* vorbereitet sind.

### Hinweise zum Bewertungssystem

Die Hinweise zur Bewertung der Leistungen haben Vorschlagscharakter. Die Aufgaben und Klassenarbeiten folgen der Zielrichtung des Englischunterrichts, die S zur Kommunikation in der englischen Sprache zu befähigen. Bei der Bewertung sind daher sowohl die sach- und adressatengerechten Aussagen (Inhalt) als auch das sprachliche Ausdrucksvermögen und die Korrektheit (Sprache) zu beurteilen.

Aufgaben des **halboffenen** und des **offenen Typs** verlangen von den Lernenden komplexe, selbstständige inhaltliche und sprachliche Leistungen. Für diese Aufgaben wird vorgeschlagen, je eine Teilnote für die inhaltliche Leistung und die sprachliche Leistung zu ermitteln, aus der sich die Gesamtnote ergibt. Der Bewertungsschlüssel akzentuiert, je nach Aufgabenstellung, den sprachlichen oder den inhaltlichen Bereich einer Teilaufgabe.

Die **inhaltliche** Leistung bezieht sich auf die sachliche Richtigkeit, die Vollständigkeit oder den Umfang der Aussagen und die gedankliche Ordnung bzw. die folgerichtige Anordnung der Inhalte (Textkohärenz). Bei einigen Aufgaben sind die Verwirklichung der kommunikativen Absicht und der gelungene Adressaten-Bezug der Aussagen zu bewerten. Es kann durchaus sinnvoll sein, Inhaltspunkte zu vergeben und diese in eine Teilnote umzusetzen. Dabei werden der Ideenreichtum und der Grad der eigenständigen Bearbeitung der Aufgaben durch Zusatzpunkte belohnt.

Die **sprachliche** Leistung setzt sich aus den beiden Komponenten Sprachrichtigkeit (Anzahl der sprachlichen Mängel im Verhältnis zum Textumfang) und Ausdrucksvermögen zusammen. Wie diese beiden Aspekte der sprachlichen Leistung zu gewichten sind, liegt im Ermessen der Lehrenden. Grundsätzlich sollten S ermutigt werden, sich ausführlich in der Fremdsprache zu äußern, auch zu Lasten der sprachlichen Richtigkeit.

Häufig wird bei der **Bildung der Gesamtnote** das Verhältnis 1 zu 1 vorgeschlagen. Je nach Vorbereitung, Schwerpunktsetzung und Lernstand der Klasse kann eine andere Gewichtung sinnvoll sein. Da hier sowohl die Lernleistung der S als auch ihr individueller Lernprozess und -fortschritt im Vordergrund stehen, wird auf eine verbindliche Angabe zu den maximal erreichbaren Punkten in diesem Bewertungsschlüssel verzichtet. Die **Lösungen** haben bei den **offenen** Aufgaben Modellcharakter. Sie können bei der Rückgabe und Besprechung der Klassenarbeiten als Mustertexte dienen, an denen z. B. die Bewertungskriterien erläutert werden. – In einigen Fällen sind als Lösungen Texte und Geschichten entstanden, die mehrere Funktionen haben können: entweder können sie vorab als Modelltexte mit den Schülerinnen und Schülern besprochen werden um zu zeigen, welche Erwartungen die Lehrerinnen und Lehrer bei der Lösung solcher Aufgaben haben. Dann jedoch können diese Aufgaben nicht mehr Teil der Klassenarbeit sein. Die Lehrerinnen und Lehrer müssten sich in diesem Fall für eine andere offene Aufgabe entscheiden. Jedoch können diese Texte auch Grundlage einer neuen Klassenarbeit sein, zu denen die Lehrerinnen und Lehrer selbst Aufgaben entwickeln. Bei den Lösungen handelt es sich jeweils um Maximalanforderungen, die die Lehrerinnen und Lehrer in dieser Form nicht erwarten dürfen.

Das Vokabular in den Lösungstexten geht zum Teil über den Wortschatz von *Password Orange Erweiterungskurs 6* hinaus. (Die neuen Wörter sind jeweils **unterstrichen**). Hier wurde dem in Klasse 10 sicherlich entwickelten individuellen Wortschatz der S Rechnung getragen. Sollten L diese Texte als Grundlage einer neuen Klassenarbeit verwenden, müsste das unterstrichene Vokabular reduziert und/oder z. B. als Fußnote angegeben werden.

### Britisches und amerikanisches Englisch

In *Password Orange Erweiterungskurs 6* wird S auch *American English* vorgestellt, z. T. in authentischen Texten. In den meisten Fällen beschränkt sich das Erlernen des *AE* auf die Wahrnehmung der andersartigen Aussprache und das Kennenlernen anderen Vokabulars. Die – nirgends schriftlich festgelegte – Übereinkunft scheint zu sein, dass S nur eine Version des Englischen beherrschen sollen, in den meisten Fällen also das *British English*. *AE* und *BE* sollten nebeneinander geduldet werden.

# TOPIC 1

| Nr. | Aufgabe/Klassenarbeit | Aufgabenform | Lernschwerpunkte |
|---|---|---|---|
| 1. | For the excitement | 1a) halboffen<br>1b) halboffen<br>2) geschlossen<br><br>3) offen<br>4) offen<br>5) offen | 1a) LV: reading for gist<br>1b) LV: reading for gist<br>2) LV: reading for detail<br>   LA: note-taking<br>3) T: analyzing the effect of the article on the reader<br>4) T: comparing the heading of the article to another heading<br>5) T: finding reasons |

**Bewertung:** Aufgabe 1a) und b) prüfen das Grobverständnis des Textes ab. Für die beiden Teilaufgaben können je genanntem inhaltlichen Aspekt 2 Punkte vergeben werden (je 1 Punkt für die sprachliche und inhaltliche Richtigkeit). In Aufgabe 2 sollte sowohl die inhaltliche als auch die sprachliche Richtigkeit jeweils mit 1 Punkt pro Teilaufgabe bewertet werden. Da die Lern- und Arbeitstechnik des *note-taking* hier gefordert wird, sollte besonderer Wert darauf gelegt werden, dass S die Informationen wirklich nur in Stichpunkten darstellen (keine ganzen Sätze). Bei Verstößen können ggf. Punkte abgezogen werden. Aufgabe 3: Die inhaltliche Note ergibt sich aus der Ausführlichkeit der Darstellung (je genanntem Aspekt können 1–2 Punkte vergeben werden). Die sprachliche Note berücksichtigt Sprachrichtigkeit, Variabilität des Wortschatzes und Kohärenz der Ausführungen. Aufgabe 4: Diese Aufgabe fordert von S das Erkennen der Unterschiede zwischen zwei Überschriften, die sich entsprechend der Art der Zeitung unterscheiden. Die Aufgabe ist anspruchsvoll und vermutlich in erster Linie von leistungsstarken S zu lösen. Die inhaltliche Bewertung sollte den Schwerpunkt der Benotung ausmachen. Als Mindestanforderung sollten S den Unterschied *information – sensation* herausstellen. Weitere Aspekte werden zusätzlich honoriert. Bei der sprachlichen Bewertung sollte die Verwendung themenspezifischen Vokabulars neben der Sprachrichtigkeit berücksichtigt werden. Aufgabe 5: Die Ausführlichkeit und Differenziertheit der Begründungen sollten bei der Bewertung des Inhalts im Mittelpunkt stehen. Die sprachliche Note ergibt sich aus der Sprachrichtigkeit und der Verwendung von strukturierendem Vokabular. Die Inhalts- und Sprachnote sollte zu gleichen Teilen in die Bewertung einfließen.

| Nr. | Aufgabe/Klassenarbeit | Aufgabenform | Lernschwerpunkte |
|---|---|---|---|
| 2. | Why did they do it? | 1) halboffen<br><br>2a) geschlossen<br>2b) geschlossen<br>3a) offen<br>3b) offen | 1) HV: listening for detail<br>   LA: note-taking<br>2a) HV: listening for detail<br>2b) HV: listening for detail<br>3a) T: paraphrasing the contents<br>3b) T: giving a judgement/giving reasons for a judgement |

**Bewertung:** Bei Aufgabe 1 und 2 a) können pro korrektem Teilaspekt 1 Punkt vergeben werden. In Teilaufgabe 2 b) können je korrekter Aussage 2 Punkte vergeben werden (inhaltliche und sprachliche Richtigkeit). Bei Aufgabe 3 handelt es sich um eine Zusammenfassung und Bewertung der Ergebnisse aus Aufgabe 1. Für die Zusammenfassung in a) können je nach Ausführlichkeit 3–6 Punkte vergeben werden. Die Sprachrichtigkeit kann ebenfalls mit entsprechenden Punktzahlen bewertet werden. In Aufgabe 3 b) wird die Ausführlichkeit und Differenziertheit auf inhaltlicher Ebene bewertet. Sprachliche Richtigkeit und die Verwendung von strukturierendem Vokabular bilden die Sprachnote.

| Nr. | Aufgabe/Klassenarbeit | Aufgabenform | Lernschwerpunkte |
|---|---|---|---|
| 3. | The old tunnel | 1) halboffen<br>2a)–d) offen<br><br>3) halboffen<br>4) geschlossen | 1) LV: reading for gist and detail<br>2a) LV: reading for detail<br>–d) T: describing the setting, key situations, characters and climax<br>3) T: writing a comment<br>4) Gr: past simple/past progressive |

**Bewertung:** In Aufgabe 1 wird das Leseverständnis überprüft. Je korrekter Satzergänzung können 2 Punkte (je 1 Punkt für sprachliche und inhaltliche Richtigkeit) vergeben werden. Die Aufgabenteile a)–d) von Aufgabe 2 beziehen sich auf die in dieser *Topic* erarbeiteten Lern- und Arbeitstechniken (*Strategy page* – SB S.16.) Inhaltlich gelten hier die korrekte Erläuterung des Analysevokabulars wie *setting, key situations* und *climax* sowie die Ausführlichkeit als Bewertungsaspekte. Die sprachliche Note setzt sich zusammen aus Sprachrichtigkeit, der Verwendung von Analysevokabular (Ausdrucksvermögen) und der Kohärenz der Darstellung. Aufgabe 3 bezieht sich ebenfalls auf die in dieser *Topic* zentralen Lern- und Arbeitstechniken (*Writing a comment: Strategy page* – SB S.16). Die vorgegebenen *phrases* haben unterstützende Funktion. Die Ausführlichkeit und Originalität der Begründungen ergeben die inhaltliche Note, die sprachliche Richtigkeit bildet den Schwerpunkt der sprachlichen Note. Sofern S sich von den Vorgaben in der *box* lösen, sollte dies entsprechend positiv bewertet werden. Aufgabe 4 bezieht sich auf die in der *Topic* behandelte Grammatik. Je korrekter Form wird 1 Punkt vergeben.

| Nr. | Aufgabe/Klassenarbeit | Aufgabenform | Lernschwerpunkte |
|---|---|---|---|
| 4. | Death in the tunnel | 1) geschlossen<br><br><br>2a) geschlossen<br>2b) geschlossen | 1) HV: listening for detail<br>   LA: note-taking<br>   T: comparing a dialogue to a picture<br>2a) HV: listening for detail<br>2b) HV: listening for detail |

**Bewertung:** Die Aufgaben 1 und 2 überpüfen das Hörverständnis. In Aufgabe 1 werden je korrekter Angabe 3 Punkte vergeben (1 Punkt für die Markierung, 2 Punkte für die Formulierung der Korrektur). Aufgabe 2: Hier handelt es sich um eine Transferleistung. S müssen nicht nur richtig und falsch aus dem Text heraus hören, sondern darüber hinaus Nicht-Gehörtes eliminieren und Gehörtes analysieren. Jede korrekte Angabe sollte daher mit 2 Punkten bewertet werden.

| Nr. | Aufgabe/Klassenarbeit | Aufgabenform | Lernschwerpunkte |
|---|---|---|---|
| 5. | Extreme sports | 1a) geschlossen<br><br>1b) geschlossen<br>2) geschlossen<br>3) offen | 1a) LV: reading for gist and detail<br>   Wo: extreme sports<br>1b) LA: quoting from a text<br>2) Gr: present perfect/past simple<br>3) Wo: extreme sports<br>   T: finding reasons/giving examples |

**Bewertung:** Aufgabe 1a) und b) überprüfen das Textverständnis. Je korrekter Zuordnung kann 1 Punkt vergeben werden. Aufgabe 2 befasst sich mit einem weiteren Grammatikbereich, der in der *Topic* wiederholt wurde. Je korrekter Verbform wird 1 Punkt vergeben. Aufgabe 3 bezieht sich auf die Problematik der *extreme sports*, die auch im Rahmen der Arbeit an den *Topic*-Texten aufgegriffen wurde. S können hier eigene Kenntnisse und Erfahrungen anhand von Beispielen einbringen. Inhaltlich sollte die Ausführlichkeit und Originalität der Ausführungen bewertet werden. Die Sprachnote setzt sich aus Sprachrichtigkeit, der Verwendung des themenspezifischen Vokabulars und der Strukturierung der Begründungen und Beispiele zusammen. Sprach- und Inhaltsnote sollten zu gleichen Teilen in die Bewertung einfließen.

# TOPIC 1

## 1 For the excitement

### Teenage Rock-throwers Kill Two in Car
*by Brian Hardwicke*

February 20, 2001

**Augsburg, Germany.** Red and white police tape[1] stops pedestrians from crossing a footbridge across the four-lane Ulm-Munich highway here in Bavaria, Germany. From this bridge three American teenagers aged 14, 17 and 18 threw volleyball-sized rocks Sunday night which hit six cars on the highway.

Two women, aged 30 and 48, were killed when a rock broke through the windshield[2] of their Toyota. It was later found in their car. Five people in other cars were hurt, too.

The policeman on duty[3] gets an important message over his cell phone[4], removes the tape and walks to his car to return to police headquarters[5] in Augsburg. "I am not allowed to give any information, there will be a press conference soon," is his only comment.

Later in the day, police officer Walter Staedler informs reporters that four teenagers have been arrested after U.S. military and German police offered a $5,000 reward for information. One teenager has been set free after police found out he had not taken part in the attacks. The three other boys admit to throwing rocks onto passing cars. Two of them are high school students who earlier told classmates about their rock-throwing activities. With this information police were able to arrest the boys in their homes. 'American Soldiers' Sons – The Killer Kids of Augsburg' was the headline in *Bild*, a popular German daily newspaper.

The car drivers didn't have any chance to escape the rocks raining down on them, so the boys face the possibility of sentences[6] of more than 10 years.

---

**1. a)** *What information do you get from the title of the newspaper article?*

_____

**b)** *In about 10–15 words write down what the article is about.*

_____

**2.** *Now read the text again. Answer the questions in note form:*

who? _____

where? _____

when? _____

what? _____

**3.** *Describe how the author of this article gets the reader's interest.*

**4.** *Compare the heading from* Bild *with the heading which was chosen for this article.*

**5.** *In his article the writer does not give any reasons for the teenagers' behaviour. Point out possible reasons.*

---

[1] **tape** – Band; [2] **windshield** – Windschutzscheibe; [3] **on duty** – im Dienst; [4] **cell phone (AE)** = mobile phone (BE);
[5] **headquarters** – Hauptquartier; [6] **sentence** – Gefängnisstrafe

TOPIC 1

## 2 Why did they do it?

1. Three teenage boys threw volleyball-sized rocks from a bridge over a four-lane highway near Augsburg. They hit six cars and two women died.
   Listen to what the three boys say about themselves and the incident[1]. Then fill in the grid.

| name | age | how he was involved in the incident (planning, throwing etc.) | what he did after the incident |
|---|---|---|---|
| Craig Smith | | | |
| Ian McDuff | | | |
| Steve Browning | | | |

2. a) Read the following statements. Say if they are (r) or wrong (w).

| | |
|---|---|
| 1. Craig was drunk when the incident happened. | |
| 2. Craig was on the bridge. | |
| 3. After the incident Ian took Craig home on his motorcycle. | |
| 4. Ian's father is an officer in the army. | |
| 5. Ian has got a job. | |
| 6. Ian thinks frightening car drivers is fun. | |
| 7. It was Ian's idea to throw stones from the bridge after he had seen a film at the cinema. | |
| 8. Steve met Ian at the officer's club. | |
| 9. Steve has got a motorcycle. | |
| 10. Ian feels sorry for Craig. | |

b) Now correct the wrong statements.

_____

_____

_____

_____

3. a) How did it come to the terrible deaths of the two women? Write a short report.

   b) According to the statements of the three boys point out who is most guilty and why.
      (Use your notes from 1.)

---
[1] incident – Vorfall

# TOPIC 1

## 3 The old tunnel

When we found the old tunnel, we knew at once that we were going to go in. There are signs everywhere in the hills behind Ferndale warning you about the tunnels but we didn't take any notice of them.
As soon as we went in, we heard the rats. You could hear their feet scratching the ground and see their little eyes in the dark. I switched on my flashlight[1]. We moved forward slowly but with our hearts beating fast. We didn't talk because of the echo. Every little sound came back a thousand times. It was freezing cold and there was this awful smell, but after a while we didn't notice it any more. The only thing that worried us was the echo of our feet on the ground. It sounded like someone was following us. Suddenly the tunnel divided. Which way should we go and how would we know the way out again? Mick took a piece of chalk[2] and marked both sides of the tunnel, so we would know which way to go when we came back.
We walked on for a while and then suddenly Amy screamed.

The echo was awful and the only thing I really wanted to do was turn and run. There was a skeleton[3] sitting on the floor – watching us with its empty eyes, its mouth open and laughing at us. We didn't feel there was much to laugh about. The bones of its legs ended in a pair of sneakers[4] – expensive ones – and its arms were crossed[5], as if for protection, in front of an expensive-looking leather[6] jacket.
Just imagine, three teenagers just looking for a safe place for a drink and a smoke who found a skeleton of someone about our own age. "I want to go back," Amy shouted. "Ack –Ack – Ack," the echo laughed at us. And we ran. "Stop," Mick shouted after a while, "a dead guy can't hurt us, can he?" And then we realised that we didn't have any idea where we were. Had we gone the right way to get out of the tunnel? Then we heard the noise, as if something big was coming towards us. "Back," Amy shouted. So we turned and ran.

**1.** *Finish the sentences to write a short storyline.*

1. The main characters of the story are _____

2. At the beginning of the story the three teenagers _____

3. The tunnel is a frightening place because _____

4. When the tunnel divides _____

5. Amy screams because _____

6. At the end of the story the teenagers _____

**2.** *Imagine you had to shoot a film of this story.*
  a) Describe the setting of the story.
  b) Point out the key situations of the story and give reasons why you think they are important.
  c) In a few sentences describe what you get to know about the main characters.
  d) Find the climax of the story and explain why this critical point moves the action in a different direction.

**3.** *Comment on the story by using the phrases in the box.*

> It's exciting …   I don't like it because …
> The most interesting moment is when …   The characters are …
> I don't understand why …   The story is dramatic because …
> The story doesn't say …

---

[1] **flashlight (AE)** = torch (BE); [2] **chalk** – Kreide; [3] **skeleton** – Skelett; [4] **sneakers (AE)** = trainers (BE); [5] **crossed** – verschränkt; [6] **leather** – Leder

**4.** John tells his parents about his adventure in the tunnel.
*Fill in the correct forms of the verbs. Use the past simple or the past progressive.*

1. We _____ (walk) along the tunnel when we _____ (hear) the rats.

2. We _____ (think) about which way to take when Mick _____ (take) out a piece of chalk and _____ (mark) both sides of the tunnel.

3. I _____ (watch) Mick when Amy suddenly _____ (shout).

4. We _____ (look) at the skeleton when Amy _____ (say) that she wanted to go back.

5. We _____ (run) when Mick _____ (stop) us.

6. We _____ (listen) to him when we suddenly _____ (hear) a terrible noise.

## 4 Death in the tunnel

**1.** In the hills behind Ferndale there are a lot of old mines. The tunnels are dangerous but kids from Ferndale often go there. Wandering around those tunnels gives them a kick. John, Mick and Amy were looking around the tunnels when they found a skeleton¹. Now they are at the Ferndale Sheriff's to report their find.
*Listen to the dialogue and look at the picture. There are six mistakes in the picture. Mark them with a cross and write down what is wrong.*

**2.** Here are some statements about the text.
   **a)** *Tick (✔) the ones which are correct.*

| | |
|---|---|
| 1. The sheriff wants to know the three kids' names and addresses. | |
| 2. He listens to Amy's report carefully at once. | |
| 3. The sheriff tells the kids that the tunnels are closed to the public. | |
| 4. He asks them if they saw someone stealing a sign. | |
| 5. The sheriff is happy that they entered the tunnel. | |
| 6. He wants them to come back with their parents the following day. | |
| 7. He wants to see them at 3.30 p.m. | |
| 8. The sheriff thinks that they are on drugs. | |
| 9. He is pleased because the kids have reported a missing person. | |

   **b)** *Correct the wrong statements.*

¹ **skeleton** – Skelett

# TOPIC 1

## 5 Extreme sports

### Base jumper falls 600 ft to death

**Los Angeles, November 17.** Hundreds of onlookers saw an experienced base jumper fall 600 ft to his death yesterday after his parachute failed to open.

John Thompson, 28, was doing a stunt for an action film in which he had to jump from a skyscraper in downtown Los Angeles. After a few seconds in free fall his parachute failed to open and the crowd saw Mr Thompson hit the ground at 50 mph.

The dead man, a member of the American Stunt Man Association, had done more than 100 jumps from high cliffs and buildings, and was a very professional and experienced jumper. He had trained for two years in France and Canada together with a group of 20 other base jumpers.

"He was the best and the fittest," his ex-coach, Jack Forbes, told our reporter on the phone last night. "I just can't believe he made a mistake." Jack Forbes, who does courses on base jumping and parachuting, said that especially young people often risk their lives. "But John wasn't one of them," he said. "He was very careful and always tried to persuade young people to do parachuting instead of base jumping because it is much safer. John did stunts for a living[1], not just for fun."

Shirley Jones, 23, one of the crowd said: "After his free fall it was obvious he was in trouble. He tried to free himself and it seemed as if he would be able to pull the cord[2] of his reserve parachute. But then the cord got tangled[3] in the still closed parachute, and the man hit the ground at a great speed."

Air cushions and safety sheets[4] which covered the ground could not save the man's life. Fireman Jim Wilkes said: "We couldn't do anything. Our rescue staff can do something if you are jumping from a five-story[5] house but not if you're falling 600 feet."

Several people who were watching were taken to the hospital and treated for shock.

Jamie White, 14, another onlooker said: "It looked great when he jumped and I waited to see his parachute open. When this didn't happen, I thought it was a trick or something. I only realised there was something wrong, when the man hit the ground and the film cameras stopped. For a minute or so nobody moved. It must have been the shock. Bad luck for the dead man, but I'd love to be a stuntman myself. Free falling must be great."

John Thompson leaves a widow[6] and two sons aged four and five years old.

**1. a)** Read the text and put the scenes from the report in the right order.
   **b)** Find phrases from the text that go with these scenes.

**2.** During his interview Jack Forbes gives some information about base jumping. *Use the present perfect or the past simple to complete the sentences.*

1. I _____ (meet) John Thompson two years ago.

2. I _____ (be) a member of the American Stunt Man Association since 1998.

3. I _____ (already/train) base jumpers for 6 years.

4. I _____ (just/hear) about John's death.

5. I can't understand his death, because he _____ (be) a careful and fit base jumper.

6. Last year John and I _____ (go) to Canada to do some more training.

7. I'm very sorry for his family. He _____ (invite) me to his wedding in 1996.

**3.** John Thompson tried to persuade young people to take up parachuting instead of base jumping. *Why do especially young people risk their lives by doing extreme sports? Write a short text. Give reasons and examples.*

---
[1] **living** – Lebensunterhalt; [2] **cord** – Schnur; [3] **to get tangled** – sich verheddern; [4] **safety sheet** – Sprungtuch;
[5] **five-story** – fünf Stockwerke hoch; [6] **widow** – Witwe

# TOPIC 2

| Nr. | Aufgabe/Klassenarbeit | Aufgabenform | Lernschwerpunkte |
|---|---|---|---|
| 1. | The mission | 1) geschlossen<br>2) offen<br>3) offen<br>4) geschlossen | 1) LV: reading for gist and detail<br>2) T: analyzing the speaker's argumentation<br>3) T: writing a dialogue (creative writing)<br>4) Wo: finding word families |
| **Bewertung:** Aufgabe 1 überprüft das Leseverständnis. Je korrekter Zuordnung wird 1 Punkt vergeben. In Aufgabe 2 wird eine Analyse der Strategien und der verwendeten Redemittel mit Zitatangabe im Dreischritt: These – Textbeleg – Analyse erwartet. In schwachen Gruppen kann die Aufgabe Schwierigkeiten bereiten. Deshalb sollte dort die inhaltliche Leistung den Schwerpunkt der Bewertung bilden. Die Ausführlichkeit und Differenziertheit der Ausführungen bilden die Inhaltsnote; Sprachrichtigkeit, Strukturierung der Aussagen und die Verwendung des angemessenen Vokabulars ergeben die Sprachnote. Das Zitieren aus dem Text als Lern- und Arbeitstechnik sollte bei der Bewertung honoriert werden. Aufgabe 3: Bei dieser kreativen Aufgabe sollte ebenfalls die inhaltliche Leistung im Zentrum der Bewertung stehen. Inhaltlich sollte deutlich werden, dass von einem der beiden Protagonisten eine Entscheidung getroffen wird. Die Originalität und die Ausführlichkeit bilden die Inhaltsnote. Sprachrichtigkeit, und das Ausdrucksvermögen (Merkmale der gesprochenen Sprache, Adressatenbezug usw.) ergeben die Sprachnote. Aufgabe 4: Diese Aufgabe bezieht sich auf einen Lernschwerpunkt der *Topic* im Bereich Wortschatzdifferenzierung u. -erweiterung. Die angegebenen Lexeme sind S bekannt, so dass zur Lösung der Aufgabe die Verwendung eines Wörterbuchs nicht unbedingt erforderlich ist, jedoch zugelassen werden kann. Je korrekter Form wird ein Punkt vergeben. ||||
| 2. | Trapped | 1a) geschlossen<br>1b) geschlossen<br>2) halboffen<br>3) offen<br>4) offen | 1a)–b) HV: listening for detail<br><br>2) HV: listening for detail<br>LA: note-taking<br>3) T: describing the inner conflict/finding solutions to a problem<br>4) T: continuing a dialogue (creative writing) |
| **Bewertung:** Aufgabe 1 und 2 überprüfen das detaillierte Hörverstehen. In Aufgabe 1 a) kann pro korrektem Aspekt 1 Punkt vergeben werden. Mängel hinsichtlich der Sprachrichtigkeit können durch Punktabzug berücksichtigt werden. In Aufgabe 1b) sollten pro richtiger Aussage je 2 Punkte vergeben werden (je 1 Punkt für Inhalt und Sprachrichtigkeit). Aufgabe 2 fordert ein intensives Hörverständnis. Ein mehrmaliges Vorspielen ist zur Erledigung dieser Aufgabe sinnvoll. Für die ersten 4 *items* werden je 1 Punkt vergeben, für die anderen Bereiche je 2 Punkte (je 1 Punkt für Inhalt und Sprachrichtigkeit), da S hier differenziertere Aussagen machen müssen. Die Aufgaben 1 und 2 können auch alternativ eingesetzt werden. Aufgabe 3: S versetzen sich in die Situation des Protagonisten. Die Verwendung der *if-clauses type 2* ist erforderlich. S sollten hier mehrere Alternativen aufzeigen, jedoch zu einem Ergebnis gelangen. Bei dieser Aufgabe sollten die Ideen der S Vorrang vor der sprachlichen Richtigkeit der Aussagen haben. Aufgabe 4 spricht die Fantasie der S an. Bei dieser kreativen Aufgabe steht die inhaltliche Leistung im Vordergrund (siehe Aufgabe 3 zu Text 1 – The Mission). S sollten zu einem Ergebnis gelangen, was das Verhalten der Protagonisten betrifft. Sinnvoll wäre es, eine Mindestanzahl (z. B. 5) von Äußerungen jedes Protagonisten vorzugeben. ||||
| 3. | Bullying in schools | 1) geschlossen<br><br>2) halboffen | 1) LV: reading for detail<br>Wo: bullying<br>LA: quoting from a text<br>2) LV: reading for detail<br>T: describing problems/finding reasons |
| **Bewertung:** In Aufgabe 1 wird das Leseverständnis überprüft. Je korrekter Zuordnung kann 1 Punkt vergeben werden. Aufgabe 2 überprüft nicht nur das Leseverstehen, sondern erfordert eine Begründung, die S mit Hilfe des Lesetextes formulieren. Je korrekter Zuordnung (bullying or not) kann 1 Punkt vergeben werden. Je nach Ausführlichkeit der Begründung werden 2–3 Punkte vergeben. Verstöße gegen die Sprachrichtigkeit können durch Punktabzug in die Bewertung einbezogen werden. ||||
| 4. | This is school, too | 1a) geschlossen<br><br>1b) offen<br><br>2a) geschlossen<br>2b) offen | 1a) HV: listening for gist and detail<br>LA: reading for detail<br>1b) T: giving one's opinion<br>T: giving reasons<br>2a) HV: listening for detail<br>2b) T: finding keywords to pictures |
| **Bewertung:** Da in Aufgabe 1a) sowohl Hör- als auch Leseverstehen überprüft werden, muss S ausreichend Zeit zur Verfügung gestellt werden. S lesen zunächst die Box, hören dann den Text (ggf. mehrmals). Da hier zwei Grundfertigkeiten gleichzeitig gefordert werden, sollten für die korrekte Zuordnung mindestens jeweils 2 Punkte vergeben werden. Aufgabe 1b) fordert die Begründung der Zuordnung aus Teilaufgabe a). In leistungsschwachen Lerngruppen kann L u. U. zur Verdeutlichung ein Beispiel (siehe Lösungen) angeben. Für die richtige Zuordnung wird je 1 Punkt vergeben, für die Begründungen je 2 Punkte. Wenn S über das Zitat der Types of bullying hinaus eine Begründung aus dem Hörtext liefern, können Zusatzpunkte gegeben werden. Aufgabe 2: Hier wird das Hörverständnis überprüft. Je korrekter Zuordnung in a) und b) kann jeweils 1 Punkt vergeben werden. ||||
| 5. | Dead boring | 1) geschlossen<br>2) offen<br><br>3) offen<br><br>4) offen | 1) LV: reading for detail<br>2) LV: reading for detail<br>T: describing parts of a film<br>3) LV: reading for detail<br>T: giving one's opinion<br>4) LA: note-taking<br>LA: collecting arguments |
| **Bewertung:** Aufgabe 1: Das Auffinden der Fehler und die Korrektur erfordern ein intensives Lesen des Textes. Bei dieser Überprüfung des Leseverständnisses können für das Finden der Fehler je 1 Punkt pro Fehler und 2 weitere Punkte (je 1 Punkt für Inhalt und Sprachrichtigkeit) für jede richtige Korrektur vergeben werden. Aufgabe 2: Die Ausführlichkeit und Originalität der Beschreibungen ergeben die inhaltliche Note. Die Sprachnote ergibt sich aus Sprachrichtigkeit, Ausdrucksvermögen und Strukturierung der Darstellung. Sprach- und Inhaltsnote sollten zu gleichen Teilen in die Bewertung eingehen. Aufgabe 3: Auf inhaltlicher Ebene wird neben der Angabe der eigenen Meinung auch die Anzahl und Logik der Argumente bewertet. Die Sprachnote setzt sich aus Sprachrichtigkeit, angemessenem Vokabular und der Verknüpfung der einzelnen Argumentationsteile zusammen. Aufgabe 4: Diese Aufgabe transferiert die Thematik des Textes in den Lebensbereich der S. Die Anzahl und Originalität der Argumente ergeben die Inhaltsnote, die Sprachnote ergibt sich aus der Sprachrichtigkeit und dem Ausdrucksvermögen. Da in dieser Aufgabe keine vollständig ausformulierte Argumentation gefordert wird, kann die Inhaltsnote den Schwerpunkt der Bewertung bilden. ||||

# TOPIC 2

## 1 The mission

*This is an extract from a novel. In it there is the racist organization 'White up' that wants to drive black people out of the city. Here John, the leader, is talking at a meeting.*

"Good evening, ladies and gentlemen. Since our time is limited, let's come straight to the point. The first thing I'd like to do tonight is to say thank you to 16-year-old Neil who did a great job last Monday.
5 I'd like to thank him for his great success. Because of this Winfield Road is ours again. Flames have cleaned that street. Empty ghetto houses. Every single black family has left. And soon all the black ghettos in the U.S.A. will have disappeared. Don't forget, we are one of the biggest
10 organizations in the United States.
We'll drive the Blacks out of our country back to where they belong – to Africa. Black faces will disappear from our stores, our schools, our streets and our cities.
Tonight it is my pleasure to give somebody else the
15 chance to help with the cleaning and tidying.
Our enemies say this is the wrong way, that integration is the way. But tell me, do you want your daughter or sister to hang around with or even to marry a person of that race?
20 Our enemies say Blacks contribute[1] to our way of living. Do they? Is there anybody in this room who believes they do? Then I want him or her to stand up and speak out! – There isn't anyone?
Is there anyone who thinks it was a mistake to burn down that house in Winfield Road? Come on! Stand up! Speak 25 out! And I promise nothing will happen to him or her! There isn't anyone?
Then I think the time has come to start something new: In this packet there is something I'd like you to see. Oh, maybe not now. It is not a bomb as you might expect. No, 30 no, but I promise, if this packet is put in the right place it will be more explosive than a bomb. But I mustn't tell you too much! There might be people among us who don't believe in us any more. There might be people among us who will contact the press or even the police. So it's 35 better not to say too much.
I'd like to ask you if we should put the packet in the right place. But I can't, because of the danger I am in, because of the danger we are all in from those who do not believe in us any more, those who are spies[2] and traitors[3]. 40
Let me ask you again. Do you agree with me that this city must be cleaned and cleared? Do you agree with me that it is only us who can do it?
Do you want us to put this packet in the right place? Yes? Are you sure? Okay then, ladies and gentlemen. I thank 45 you for coming. Have a nice evening. I'd like Ron, Susan and George to stay here for a moment. Thank you and good night."

1. Put the sentences in the correct order (A–G) to make a summary of this speech.

| | |
|---|---|
| 1. The speaker thanks a member of the organization because he has burned down a house in a street where Blacks live. | |
| 2. He asks his audience if the attack was wrong. | |
| 3. At the end of his speech he asks the audience to agree with the next attack, says good-bye and asks some of the members to meet him after the meeting. | |
| 4. After that he deals with the arguments that the enemies of 'White up' have against the organization's aims. | |
| 5. Then he points out that the organization is in danger from people who don't agree with its aims and who turn to newspapers and the authorities. | |
| 6. He mentions the aim of the organization, which is to send black people back to the continent they once came from. | |
| 7. After he has noted that no one is against their attacks he says that a new mission is planned against Blacks. | |

2. Describe how the speaker persuades his audience to believe that the organization 'White Up' is doing the right thing.

3. Write a short dialogue between John, Ron, Susan and George to continue the story.

4. The following words from the text are part of word families. Make a grid and find words to complete the list.

**verbs:** to think, to forget, to speak, to like, to thank, to disappear
**nouns:** success, danger, pleasure
**adjective:** explosive

| verb | noun | adjective |
|---|---|---|
| | | |

---
[1] **to contribute** – beitragen; [2] **spy** – Spion; [3] **traitor** – Verräter

# TOPIC 2

 **2 Trapped**

1. a) *Listen to the dialogue then find out if the following statements are right (r) or wrong (w) or if no information (n.i.) is given.*

| | |
|---|---|
| 1. Neil wants to leave the organization 'White Up'. | |
| 2. John tells him that there is a rule which says that no one can leave 'White Up'. | |
| 3. Neil has been a member of the organization for two years now. | |
| 4. Neil can't come to the meeting that night because he has got an English assignment to do. | |
| 5. John says it is okay that Neil can't come that evening. | |
| 6. Neil is 16 years old. | |
| 7. Other members of the group wanted John to kick out Neil. | |
| 8. Neil says he'll tell his teacher about what he did. | |
| 9. Neil used gasoline to burn down the house. | |
| 10. John wants Neil to meet him in front of the supermarket at 7 o'clock. | |

b) *Correct the wrong statements.*

2. *Write down all the information you get from the text about Neil and the situation he is in.*

| name | | age | |
|---|---|---|---|
| job | | | |
| name of organization he belongs to | | | |
| what Neil has done | | | |
| reason why Neil wants to leave | | | |
| what members of the group said against Neil | | | |
| John says he'll do this if Neil leaves | | | |
| what Neil offers to do | | | |
| what John orders[1] Neil to do at the end of the conversation | | | |

3. *Think about Neil's inner conflict – what would you do if you were in his position?*

4. *What will happen next? Continue the dialogue.*

[1] **to order** – befehlen

© Ernst Klett Verlag GmbH, Stuttgart 2001.

11

# TOPIC 2

## 3 Bullying in schools

**1. The situation**
Thousands of kids all over the United Kingdom are bullied every day. Although there are a lot of organizations that offer help, students who are bullied are not informed about their rights.

**2. What is bullying?**
Bullying means that one student or a group of students feels stronger than the student who is bullied. Bullying is not something that happens just once, the actions against a student happen again and again and are planned.

- **What schools can do**
No law says that schools have to stop bullying, but the government asks schools to stop and punish[1] bullies. It encourages teachers to deal with bullying, even if it happens outside school. The government also asks schools to
– make rules against bullying.
– inform students, parents and teachers that bullying will not be tolerated.
– inform students what to do and where to go if they are bullied.
– train teachers and students to recognize the first signs of bullying.

- **What students can do**
Students should
– inform their parents.
– make a list of bullying incidents[2] and write down the names of the students involved in the bullying.
– complain to their teachers and ask them for help.
– write down what the teachers plan to do to stop the bullies.
– go to their headteacher if bullying continues.

- **Further help**
If all this does not help, students can write a letter of complaint to the school board[3]. They should get an answer within[4] three weeks. But students can also get help by law, because some types of bullying – such as threats[5] or physical attacks – are crimes[6]. In Scotland you can even go to the police about bullying.

**1.** *Read the following statements, then say which sentence in the text they go with.*

**A** I have been bullied for two years now, but I don't know where I can get help.

**B** For the last two months my things have 'disappeared'. I found my school bag on top of the lockers, my jacket was in a tree and my trainers were in the paper basket.

**C** There was a workshop for teachers and students last week about the process of bullying, about how a bully starts and why it's difficult to stop him/her.

**D** At the police station: "I'd like to report John Cane and Michael West. They have been hitting my son on the way to school."

**E** There is this boy, Duncan, at my school and he has got a lot of friends. And they only seem to feel cool if they can bully smaller kids.

**F** Mrs Brown is the person to go to if you've got problems with your classmates. Go and see her, she'll help you with those bullies.

**G** In our article we've given advice to students who are bullied.

**2.** *Look at the list of types of bullying. Are these students really talking about bullying?.*

**Types of bullying**

| ① teasing | ➔ | bullies make fun of you all the time |
| ② name calling | ➔ | bullies call you bad names |
| ③ spreading gossip | ➔ | bullies tell bad stories about you |
| ④ physical threats | ➔ | bullies hit or kick you |
| ⑤ attacks of any kind | ➔ | bullies hide, throw away or break your things |
| ⑥ being forced to do | ➔ | bullies make you do things you do not something want to do e.g. stealing from shops |
| ⑦ intimidation | ➔ | bullies frighten you so that e.g. you are afraid to go to school |

**Ray:** They threw my bike into the river. I think it was because I told Mr Shepherd that Jim was trying to cheat during our test.

**Nicholas:** I know I've been missing classes for weeks, but it's these kids. They told me they would do things to me if I ever came to school again.

**Shirley:** I want to complain about John. He hid my anorak. He doesn't usually do things like that, but I was really angry because I had to go home quickly.

**Sammy:** I don't know what to do. You see, there is this story going round that I'm pregnant. But of course, I'm not! I think it started three months ago when I finished with Jim.

---

[1] **to punish** – bestrafen; [2] **incident** – Vorfall; [3] **school board** – Schulbehörde; [4] **within** – innerhalb; [5] **threat** – Drohung; [6] **crime** – Verbrechen

© Ernst Klett Verlag GmbH, Stuttgart 2001.

# TOPIC 2

 **4 This is school, too**

1. a) *Look at the list of types of bullying. Listen to Jeremy and Natalie, then say which of the items in the box go with their stories.*
   b) *Choose three of the types from the list and explain why you think they fit Natalie's or Jeremy's story.*

2. *Listen to Jeremy and Natalie again.*
   a) *Put the pictures in the right order (A–F) according to the texts you hear.*
   b) *Write a keyword from the text for each of the pictures.*

Jeremy:

_____   _____   _____

_____   _____   _____

Natalie:

_____   _____   _____

_____   _____   _____

© Ernst Klett Verlag GmbH, Stuttgart 2001.

# TOPIC 2

## 5 Dead boring

You see, I had met this boy, Pedro, and it was Monday morning, Social Studies – dead boring, if you ask me. It was October, the year 2038, the sun was shining, and Mrs Wright's voice was going on and on, talking about
5 immigrants to our country. And it wasn't the first time (yawn[1], yawn). We were doing revision for our exams in November. I switched off, thinking of something – well someone – quite different.

Mrs Wright was talking about this bill[2] of restrictions[3] to
10 stop Mexicans coming into our country, and I wasn't listening. Suddenly she stopped talking and asked: "Why did the government introduce this bill of restrictions, Sheila Alington?" Sheila Alington, that's me.

"What restrictions, Miss?" I asked. "Well, the restrictions
15 I've been talking about for the last half hour," she said coldly, "while you were looking out the window."

"No idea!" I said, and you could see, she didn't like my answer. The class was dead quiet. And so was she. I expected her to scream, but she didn't. Then she started
20 speaking slowly and clearly as if we were having a dictation: "These restrictions were made to stop the part of the population which gave least to society from living on American money and from infiltrating America with their way of life. Do you think you can remember that?" "Yes,25 miss," I said. She looked at me like a shark. "Well, I hope you can," she went on, "because when you go home, you will write it down 30 times, that's once for each minute you've wasted in my class."

You won't believe it, but I did it. I wrote those lines 30 times 30 when I got home from school. And while I was writing I realized WHAT I was writing. Pedro is Mexican. His family came to this country 10 years ago – legally. Pedro's parents are hard-working people. They pay taxes[4] just like my parents do. And my great-grandparents came from 35 somewhere in Europe a long time ago. So why haven't we been 'infiltrating' America with our way of life?

I took my sheets[5] of paper and wrote across all of them: *'All human beings are born free and equal in dignity[6] and rights.'* And *'Everyone is entitled[7] to all the rights ...* 40 *without distinction[8] ... such as race, color, national or social origin ...'*.

You want to know what happened? I got thrown out of school, just for writing out article 1 and 2 of the Universal Declaration[9] of Human Rights, 1948. 45

1. *Frank, a student at Wilmington High, had to sum up this text. He made nine mistakes. Find them and correct them.*

> At the beginning of the story a girl tells us about a Social Studies lesson which she liked because they were talking about immigrants to the U.S.A. But then she starts to think about Pedro, a Spanish boy who she met on Monday morning. Her teacher Mrs Wright notices that she is dreaming and gives her some extra homework. Sharon has to copy some lines from the Universal Declaration of Human Rights.
> After school she writes the lines 20 times. But while she is doing that, she realizes that the restrictions are wrong, because her boyfriend's family came to the U.S.A. legally a short time ago and because they pay taxes. She can't understand why her family isn't infiltrating the U.S.A. because her great-grandparents came from Australia. So she throws her lines away. At the end of the story she gets thrown out of school.

2. *Imagine this story is part of a film. Use the information in the text and describe the scenes and the action. You can complete the description by adding your own ideas for the details.*

3. *After Sheila gets expelled from school, some people are interviewed by a reporter. Here is what they say. Read the comments, choose one and say why you agree or disagree with it.*

> **Pedro:** When Sheila told me what had happened I knew at once it was all my fault. If she had not been going around with me, she would have been okay, wouldn't she?

> **Mother:** Sheila has changed ever since she met that Mexican boy. We'll send her to a private school. It will do her a lot of good to be with the right sort of kids.

> **Teacher:** Sheila Alington? ... Oh, yes. She was such a nice girl. I just don't know what has come over her.

> **Grandmother:** Sheila has spoken out for everybody's rights. That stupid teacher should be expelled.

> **Friend:** My parents don't want me to see a lot of Sheila now, and up to a certain point I agree. Most foreigners get into trouble, don't they?

4. *What do you think about restrictions on immigrants to your country? Collect pros and cons in a list.*

---

[1] **to yawn** – gähnen; [2] **bill** – Gesetz; [3] **restriction** – Einschränkung; [4] **tax** – Steuer; [5] **sheet** – Blatt; [6] **dignity** – Würde;
[7] **to be entitled to** – berechtigt sein; [8] **distinction** – Unterschied; [9] **declaration** – Erklärung

# TOPIC 3

| Nr. | Aufgabe/Klassenarbeit | Aufgabenform | Lernschwerpunkte |
|---|---|---|---|
| 1. | Addicted to the Internet | 1) offen<br>2a) geschlossen<br>2b) offen<br>2c) offen<br>3) offen<br>4) geschlossen | 1) LV: reading for gist and detail; T: paraphrasing the contents<br>2a) Wo: computer; LV: reading for detail<br>2b) Wo: computer<br>2c) Wo/Wi: computer; T: giving definitions/explanations<br>3) LA: quoting from the text; T: analyzing the main character<br>4) Gr: present simple/present progressive |
| **Bewertung:** In Aufgabe 1 wird neben der Überprüfung des Textverständnisses auch Abstraktionsvermögen von den S erwartet. Hier sollte die inhaltliche Richtigkeit und Prägnanz der Aussagen stärker bewertet werden als die Sprachrichtigkeit und das Ausdrucksvermögen. Aufgabe 2 bezieht sich auf den in der *Topic* vermittelten Wortschatz. Bei den Teilaufgaben a) und b) wird je korrektem Begriff 1 Punkt vergeben, bei c) können je nach Ausführlichkeit der Erklärung 2–3 Punkte gegeben werden (bei Mängeln bzgl. Sprachrichtigkeit werden weniger Punkte vergeben). Aufgabe 3: Bei dieser Aufgabe kommt es darauf an, alle Textaussagen in den *extracts* zu finden, die eine Aussage über Karens Computersucht zulassen. Es wird erwartet, dass S neben der reinen Auflistung der Textstellen auch eine Begründung abgeben. Neben der Sprachrichtigkeit sollte dann vor allem auch die Verwendung von *connectives* positiv bewertet werden. Aufgabe 4 bezieht sich auf die in der *Topic* bearbeitete Grammatik. Je korrekter Form wird 1 Punkt vergeben. ||||
| 2. | A meeting with Phil | 1) geschlossen<br>2) offen<br>3) offen | 1) HV: listening for gist and detail<br>2) HV: listening for gist and detail<br>T: paraphrasing the contents of a dialogue<br>3) T: analyzing the main character's plan of action |
| **Bewertung:** In leistungsschwachen Lerngruppen wird ggf. ein mehrmaliges Vorspielen des Dialoges notwendig sein, damit S Aufgabe 1 bewältigen können. Für das Erfassen der richtigen Reihenfolge wird je Satz 1 Punkt vergeben. Aufgabe 2 kann entweder alternativ oder ergänzend zu Aufgabe 1 bearbeitet werden. Bei der Bewertung wird inhaltlich der Schwerpunkt auf die Richtigkeit der Aussagen gelegt, die Sprachnote ergibt sich aus Sprachrichtigkeit und Ausdrucksvermögen. Aufgabe 3: Diese Aufgabe setzt sich bzgl. des Anspruchsniveaus von den Aufgabe 1 und 2 ab. S müssen die Vorgehensweise Phils durchschauen. Die Sprachnote ergibt sich aus Sprachrichtigkeit, Ausdrucksvermögen und Strukturierung der Darstellung und sollte weniger gewichtet werden als die inhaltliche Leistung. ||||
| 3. | Work experience at British Airways | 1a) geschlossen<br>1b) halboffen | 1a) Wi: structure of formal letters<br>1b) LA/T: writing a formal letter |
| **Bewertung:** Bei den Aufgaben 1 und 2 werden die in der *Topic* geübten Lern- und Arbeitstechniken aufgegriffen. In Aufgabe 1 geht es um eine Überprüfung der Kenntnisse zu Formalien eines Bewerbungsschreibens. Hier kann je korrekter Einordnung 1 Punkt vergeben werden. In Aufgabe 2 formulieren S mit Hilfe der in den *mails* gegebenen Informationen einen formellen Brief. Bei der Bewertung sollte neben inhaltlicher und sprachlicher Richtigkeit vor allem die Beachtung der Formalien (Aufbau des formellen Briefes siehe auch *Strategy page* – SB S. 49) einbezogen werden. ||||
| 4. | Is Tupac still alive? | 1) geschlossen<br>2) offen<br>3) offen<br>4) offen | 1) LV: listening for detail<br>LA: note-taking<br>2) LV: reading for detail<br>T: asking questions/finding answers to questions<br>3) T: finding arguments<br>4) LA: collecting ways of how to get information |
| **Bewertung:** Aufgabe 1 überprüft das Leseverständnis. Pro korrekter Erklärung zu der Skizze sollten je nach Umfang 1–2 Punkte vergeben werden. Aufgabe 2: Sowohl bei der Formulierung der Fragen als auch bei den Antworten sollten Originalität (Inhaltsnote) und sprachliche Differenziertheit/Ausdrucksvermögen (Sprachnote) den Schwerpunkt der Bewertung bilden. Aufgabe 3: Auf der Grundlage der beiden Texte und evtl. eigenen Kenntnissen finden S 3 Argumente. Hier sollte die Ausführlichkeit und Originalität zur Inhaltsnote führen, Sprachrichtigkeit, Ausdrucksvermögen und Strukturierung der Darstellung ergeben die Sprachnote. Sprache und Inhalt sollten zu gleichen Teilen in die Bewertung einfließen. In Aufgabe 4 zeigen S Möglichkeiten der Informationsbeschaffung auf. Die Ausführlichkeit und Korrektheit der Angaben ergeben die Inhaltsnote, die Sprachrichtigkeit und die Verwendung adäquaten Vokabulars bilden die Sprachnote. Alternativ werden je korrekter Angabe 2 Punkte vergeben (je 1 Punkt für Inhalt und Sprache). ||||
| 5. | The key to the future | 1a) geschlossen<br>1b) geschossen<br>1c) halboffen<br>2) halboffen<br>3) offen<br>4) offen<br>5a) geschlossen<br>5b) offen | 1a)–c) LA: looking for detail<br>LA: describing a picture/an advertisement<br>2) LV: reading for detail<br>T: paraphrasing the contents<br>3) T: analyzing the headline<br>4) LA: analyzing a picture<br>T: describing the message<br>5a) Gr: adverbs of frequency<br>5b) T: describing one's own habits |
| **Bewertung:** Aufgabe 1 erfordert eine Beschreibung der Abbildung. S müssen dazu die Details der Abbildung erfassen und versprachlichen. Bei den Teilaufgaben a) und b) sollten je korrekter Aussage 2 Punkte (je 1 Punkt für Inhalt und Sprache) vergeben werden. Aufgabenteil c) geht über die Beschreibung hinaus und erwartet Ansätze von Analyse. Hier können je nach Ausführlichkeit der Erklärung mehr Punkte gegeben werden. Aufgabe 2 überprüft das Leseverstehen. Bei der Beantwortung kommt es darauf an, dass S die Informationen wirklich zusammenfassen und nicht einfach aus der Anzeige abschreiben. Dies sollte bei der Bewertung besonders beachtet werden. Aufgabe 3: Die Interpretation der Überschrift kann schwächeren S möglicherweise Schwierigkeiten bereiten. Da dies für sie eine inhaltliche Herausforderung darstellt, sollte der Schwerpunkt der Bewertung im inhaltlichen Bereich liegen. Die Ausführlichkeit/Differenziertheit der Argumentation stellt den Schwerpunkt der Inhaltsnote dar. Die sprachliche Leistung bezieht sich auf die Verwendung angemessenen Vokabulars, Strukturierung der Aussagen und die Sprachrichtigkeit. In schwächeren Lerngruppen können Inhalt und Sprache bei dieser Aufgabe durchaus im Verhältnis 70% zu 30% bewertet werden. Aufgabe 4: Da es sich bei dieser Aufgabe um eine Transferleistung handelt, sollte die inhaltliche Ausführlichkeit und Differenziertheit stärker bewertet werden, als die sprachliche Leistung (Sprachrichtigkeit, Ausdrucksvermögen, Strukturierung). Aufgabe 5a) bezieht sich auf die in der *Topic* bearbeitete Grammatik *(adverbs of frequency)*. Je korrekt eingesetzm Adverb können 1–2 Punkte vergeben werden. Bei Teilaufgabe b) beschreiben S ihre eigenen Gewohnheiten. Ausführlichkeit und Prägnanz bestimmen die Inhaltsnote, Sprachrichtigkeit und Ausdrucksvermögen die Sprachnote. Inhalts- und Sprachnote gehen im Verhältnis 60% zu 40% in die Endnote ein. ||||

# TOPIC 3

## 1 Addicted[1] to the Internet

Here are extracts from two diaries – Karen's and her mother's.

**Karen**

**September 7th, 4 a.m.**
Just read the last two pages in my diary. Can hardly believe I was so excited about all those people I met on the Internet.
This has been the worst night of my life. Everything started off okay. Chatted with Nat for a while, but then he said he had work to do. Liar[2]! Didn't know who to contact next. Got onto Duncan, but he told me to wait. So I did. Then got disconnected and tried Nat again. He was still in the chat room. But not with me!!
Then Mum came in with something in her hand. Shouted at me to switch the awful thing (the computer) off. I didn't want to. Then Dad came in. Shouting. Still don't know what he was talking about.

**September 8th, 3 a.m.**
Dead tired. Nobody talked to me at the breakfast table. Found a telephone bill on my plate for £900!! It can't be that much. In the afternoon parents – angry, talked to me and told me I had to pay the £900! I have to sell the computer (!!!), find a job and pay back the money. No pocket money until everything is paid! They have taken my computer away. But I need it, I must find another one.

**September 9th, 6 p.m.**
Am in London. With Duncan. He wasn't happy to see me, because he is living with his girlfriend, Nina. But at least she was nice and understanding[3]. She let me stay, but am not allowed to use their computer! What am I going to do? Nina made me write an e-mail to my parents saying that I was okay.

**Mum**

**September 7th, 10.30 p.m.**
Karen is obsessed with the Internet. I'm sure of it. I didn't know what to do when I saw that telephone bill: £900!! We can't afford it. Why did I agree to give her the computer as a Christmas present? But how was I to know she would use the damn thing night after night? Karen isn't herself any more. When I went into her room and asked her to turn the computer off she simply ignored me. I started shouting at her, but it didn't help. So I asked Peter to talk to her, but he didn't get through to her either.

**September 8th, 6.00 p.m.**
I am really worried. We didn't say a word to Karen this morning. She is usually terribly worried if we don't speak to her, but she has changed. It is as if she was on drugs. Maybe these chat rooms are a sort of drug. They must be. My friendly and optimistic daughter looks and behaves like a zombie. She moves differently, she hardly eats, she doesn't talk to us any more. I don't really know if she realizes the amount of money her Internet hobby costs. About an hour ago we tried to talk to her. We had a fight and Peter went mad[4] and said she had to sell the computer. Of course she can't pay all the money back. In the end she banged her bedroom door and locked it. There is something going on in that room of hers. Peter tried to talk to her. No answer!

**September, 9th, 4 p.m.**
Karen has run away! I know because she has taken her diary and £150 is missing from my purse. I phoned her cousin, Phil. He was sweet and came round at once. He went onto the Internet for us and found out about her Internet friends. There are 120! Where is my daughter? What am I going to tell everybody? We'll have to go to the police and report her missing. Peter told me not to worry so much. But it didn't help. Maybe we can try to find her over the Internet.

1. *Summarize the extracts from Karen's and her mother's diaries in no more than ten sentences.*

2. a) *Find words from the text that have to do with the computer.*
   b) *Add ten more computer words you know.*
   c) *Take five of the words and explain their meanings.*

3. *Karen's mother thinks that the Internet is like a drug for her daughter. Find words and phrases from both extracts that show that Karen is addicted.*

---

[1] **to be addicted to** – süchtig nach etwas sein; [2] **liar** – Lügner; [3] **understanding** – verständnisvoll; [4] **to go mad** – ausrasten

**4. A night with Karen before she ran off to London.** *Complete the text using the present simple or the present progressive.*

1. It's 5 o'clock in the evening. Karen _____ (to sit) in front of her computer.

2. She _____ (to try) to get through to Nat, who she secretly[1] _____ (to love).

3. But he _____ (to talk) to somebody else. Karen is disappointed.

4. Then she _____ (to get) through to Val, an Internet girlfriend.

5. Val _____ (to tell) Karen that Nat _____ (to talk) to Val's friend Kirsty.

6. Val knows that because Kirsty _____ (not answer) the phone at the moment.

7. Val also _____ (to write) that Kirsty _____ (to plan) a date with Nat for the coming weekend.

8. Karen is furious and _____ (to decide) not to try Nat again.

## 2 A meeting with Phil

1. Karen has been surfing on the Internet day and night for months. When her parents get a £900 phone bill, Karen has a huge argument with them and runs away from home. Her 21-year-old cousin Phil, who showed her how to use the Internet, gets an e-mail from Karen. She wants to talk to him. They meet in a cafe – somewhere in London.
   *Listen to the dialogue then put the following sentences in the right order. (Put the numbers in the box.)*

   ☐ ☐ ☐ ☐ ☐ ☐ ☐ ☐ ☐ ☐

   1. He tells her chat rooms are a way of making money.
   2. Phil tells Karen that you can pay a monthly flat rate instead of the high telephone costs.
   3. Karen is late because she wanted to see if Phil was alone.
   4. Phil promises to show Karen all about chat rooms as soon as they get home.
   5. Phil offers Karen his sandwich.
   6. Karen agrees to go home but she is worried what her parents will say.
   7. Karen informs Phil that she can't stop going online.
   8. The only thing Karen wants from Phil is money.
   9. Karen learns that there are people whose job it is to keep people in chat rooms.
   10. But Phil wants to talk to Karen.

2. *In a few sentences summarize the meeting between Karen and Phil. Start like this:*
   Karen meets her cousin Phil in a cafe in London. She pretends that she wants to meet him because …

3. *Phil persuades Karen to go home. How does he use the meeting to do it?*

---

[1] **secretly** – ins Geheim

# TOPIC 3

## 3 Work experience at British Airways

Kevin and Paul are e-mail pen friends.

---

von: Kevin Wegemann
an: Paul Smith <paulsmith@aol-online.uk>
gesendet: Freitag, 16. Februar 2001, 12.23
Betreff: application for work experience

Dear Paul,
Thank you very much for the information about work experience at British Airways. And thanks for the address. It's PO Box 125634, London W12 3PT, isn't it?
It would be great to work at their office in London. My summer holidays start on June 30th, and I'd like to start working shortly after that. Two months in London, imagine that! I know I won't be back for the first week of school
5   in August, but that shouldn't be a big problem, although I'll miss the beginning of my special courses in English and Information Technology. What's a week? – I'll catch up[1] easily and it won't be a problem for my school, especially if I can show that my English will improve a lot.
Do you think it's a good idea to tell British Airways that I'd like to study Information Technology after my A-levels[2]? And what about my two-week work experiences in Years 9 and 10? For those I worked at a computer shop and at a
10   travel agency. Should I mention that? Do you think I can ask British Airways to help me find somewhere to stay? I know I have to enclose my CV and a copy of my last report (Oops! Not too good!). Do you think they will take me in spite of that?
Before I forget: we've moved house. My new address is Schlosshofstr. 43, 33615 Bielefeld. Fortunately we can keep our telephone number: 0521/64374.
15   So now I've got to write a formal letter in English to British Airways, but I don't really know how to do it any more. We learnt all about formal letters at school a couple of years ago and I've forgotten nearly everything.
Could you help me write the letter? I'll make up for[3] it in the summer. Okay?
Thanks a lot and give my love to everybody.
Kevin
20   PS: How do you start and end a formal letter like that?

---

from: Paul Smith <paulsmith@aol-online.uk>
to: Kevin Wegemann kewegemann@web.de
sent: Monday, February 19, 2001, 9:03
subject: formal letter

Hi Kevin!
No problem! We've been doing formal letters in Computers at school for the last two years (God, how boring!). You've got all the facts, but tell British Airways that you think it'd be a good idea to experience a little of their world of work.
Now, here is your letter.

---

1. Kevin's formal letter to British Airways will have twelve parts.
   a) *Look at the parts of the letter in the box. Put them in the right order.*

   | polite ending ☐ | what Kevin expects the company to do ☐ | the date ☐ |

   signature ☐   why Kevin is writing ☐   name and address of the company Kevin is writing to ☐

   what is sent with the letter ☐   how Kevin addresses the person he is writing to ☐

   formal ending ☐   Kevin's address ☐   what qualifications Kevin has got for the job ☐

   when Kevin wants to start and finish working and why he wants to get the job ☐

   b) *Write the formal letter which Kevin got from Paul. (Make sure that your letter contains all the important parts of a formal letter mentioned in exercise a).*

---

[1] **to catch up** – aufholen; [2] **A-levels** – Abitur; [3] **to make up for** – ausgleichen

# TOPIC 3

## 4  Is Tupac still alive?

**Las Vegas, Nevada. Friday, September 13, 1996.**
At 4:03 p.m. this afternoon 'Gangsta' rapper Tupac Shakur was pronounced[1] dead at University Medical Center in Las Vegas. He died from wounds he suffered six days ago in a car-to-car shooting on a busy street a few blocks off the Las Vegas Strip.
Shakur and Death Row Records president Marion 'Suge' Knight were shot on September 7 while Knight was driving Shakur on East Flamingo Road. They were on their way to a charity concert to collect money to keep children away from violence[2], when suddenly a white Cadillac drove up next to them on the right side of the car. A gunman fired his gun into the passenger side of Knight's car.
Tupac was shot four times in the chest[3], but Knight only received a small head wound. Thirteen shots were fired at the car Shakur was in. He was taken to the hospital soon after and had the first of three operations. It was the second time Shakur had been shot. In 1994 he was shot five times during a robbery at a Manhattan recording studio.
Knight was able to leave University Medical Center on September 8 and three days later he spoke to Metro Police, but couldn't give any information to lead police to the gunman. Las Vegas police are trying to find out who shot Shakur, but friends of the family say they know who killed him.

**Is Tupac still alive?**
After Tupac Shakur's death a lot of questions were asked and his fans didn't believe that he was really dead. In her book 'The Killing of Tupac Shakur' reporter Cathy Scott looks into these questions:
- There were about ten cars in Tupac's group, in some of them were his bodyguards. But none of them went after the white Cadillac from which he was shot.
- The white Cadillac was never found, nor were his murderers. Police did not send helicopters to go after the Cadillac.
- 'Suge' Knight, who was in the car when Tupac was shot, has never talked about Tupac's death to the press.
- Tupac used to wear a bullet-proof vest[4]. Why didn't he wear one the day he was shot?
- Shortly before his death Tupac talked about finishing his career and disappearing from public view.
- Tupac's video 'I Ain't Mad At Cha' predicts[5] his own death.
- Tupac had read a lot of books by and about Macchiavelli who faked[6] his own death to trick his enemies.

However, Scott comes to the conclusion[7] that Tupac Amaru Shakur died. But his sad fans still think that he is alive.

1. *Take information from the texts and complete the notes to this police drawing of the shooting.*

   date: September 7, 1996
   1    East Flamingo Road
   2    ...
   3    ...

2. In her book reporter Cathy Scott comes to the conclusion that Tupac died September 13, 1996. *Look at the text, then find at least five questions which are still unanswered today. Answer these questions. (You can say what you know or what you think)*

3. *Read the last sentence of the text ('But his sad fans still think that he is alive.'). Then think of reasons why Tupac Shakur's fans don't want to accept that he is dead.*

4. You want to get more information about Tupac Amaru Shakur. *Explain the different ways you can find out more about him.*

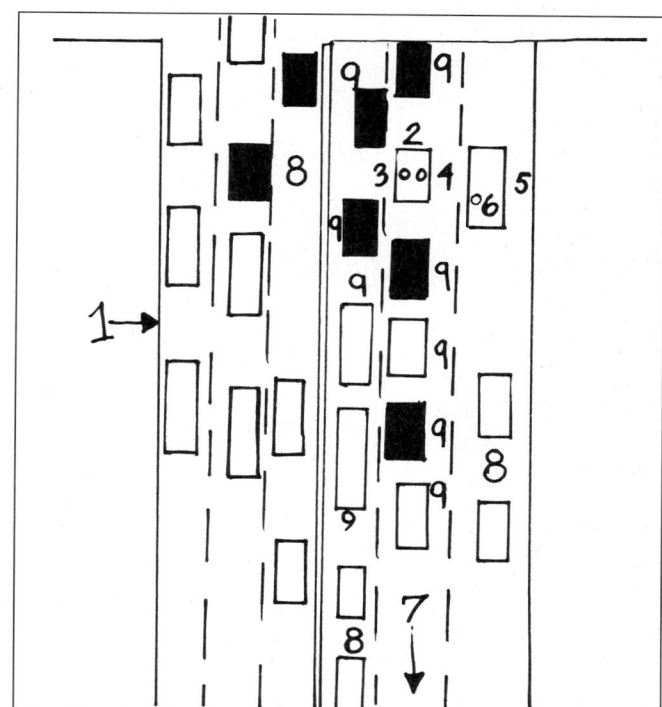

---
[1] **to pronounce** – erklären; [2] **violence** – Gewalt; [3] **chest** – Brust; [4] **bullet-proof vest** – kugelsichere Weste; [5] **to predict** – voraussagen; [6] **to fake** – vortäuschen; [7] **conclusion** – Schlussfolgerung

# TOPIC 3

## 5 The key to the future

Looking for new ideas? KEY from Calyafone can send your horoscope to your mobile phone whenever you need it – every day if you like. You won't have to pay anything for a year – that's something you can be sure of. Interested in headlines, news, weather reports, sports and lottery results? No problem, you can receive them all. And KEY will be your personal reminder, too.
All Calyafone customers can make use of KEY on their existing phones.
To register visit www.key.co.uk or call 07676067067
Full offer terms[1] and conditions available at www.key.co.uk

**KEY**
The key to success and happiness

key.co.uk from calyafone

1. Look at the picture in the advertisement, then write in a few sentences
   a) what the businessman and the gypsy are doing,
   b) what is advertised,
   c) what the glass ball and the playing cards stand for.

2. Read the text, then say in a few sentences what the company is offering.

3. Look at the headline of this advertisement, 'Key is ready'. Say why you think it was chosen.

4. With this picture what messages does Calyaphone want to present to customers?

5. a) What do these people tell you about mobile phones? Put the adverbs of frequency in the right places.

> In the 1980s there weren't any mobile phones. Doctors, firemen and policemen used walkie-talkies (always).
> **Linda**

> Then, in the beginning of the 90s businessmen used mobile phones (sometimes).
> And in the mid 90s especially young men carried them around, even if they used them (never).
> **Sue**

> I switch it off (sometimes). It's awful if you get a call in the middle of a lesson or during a meeting with somebody.
> **Pete**

> Yes, but they didn't reach very far, only a few miles (often).
> **John**

> What could I do without my mobile phone? I've got it with me and I go out without it (always/never).
> **Kirsty**

b) And you? How often do you use your mobile phone?

---
[1] **prediction** – Voraussage; [2] **term** – Zahlungsbedingung

# TOPIC 4

| Nr. | Aufgabe/Klassenarbeit | Aufgabenform | Lernschwerpunkte |
|---|---|---|---|
| 1. | I believe in you! | 1) halboffen<br><br>2) offen<br><br>3) offen<br>4) geschlossen | 1) LV: reading for detail<br>   LA: note-taking<br>   T: completing a time chart<br>2) T: describing key situations<br>   Wo: relationships<br>3) T: writing a story (creative writing)<br>4) Gr: future progressive/future perfect |
| | **Bewertung:** Aufgabe 1 überprüft das Leseverständnis. Pro Eintrag in die Tabelle können je nach Umfang 1–2 Punkte vergeben werden. Zusätzliche Informationen, die nicht aus dem Text hervorgehen, sollten mit mindestens 2 Punkten bewertet werden, da S hierzu keine sprachlichen Vorgaben im Text finden. Aufgabe 2: Bei dieser Aufgabe stehen Ausführlichkeit und Differenziertheit der Darstellung im Vordergrund der inhaltlichen Bewertung. Die Sprachnote ergibt sich aus der Sprachrichtigkeit, der Prägnanz der Formulierungen und der Strukturierung der Darstellung. Inhalts- und Sprachnote sollten gleichgewichtig in die Bewertung einfließen. Aufgabe 3: Sofern S hilflos scheinen, da sie keine eigenen Erfahrungen haben, sollte L erklären, dass S eine Geschichte erfinden können. Inhaltlich wird vor allem die Originalität und die Ausführlichkeit der Darstellung bewertet. Hinsichtlich der Sprache werden neben Sprachrichtigkeit die Struktur und die angemessene Verknüpfung der Geschehnisse bewertet. In schwachen Lerngruppen kann es ggf. sinnvoll sein, den Inhalt bei der Bewertung stärker zu berücksichtigen als die Sprache. (Frustration wegen schlechter Sprachnote würde die Bereitschaft zum kreativen Umgang mit der Sprache mindern). Aufgabe 4: Die Übung greift die in der *Topic* behandelten grammatikalischen Strukturen *(future progressive/future perfect)* auf. Je korrekt eingesetzter Form wird 1 Punkt vergeben. | | |
| 2. | The key to a happy marriage | 1) geschlossen<br><br><br>2) offen<br><br>3) offen<br><br><br>4) geschlossen | 1) LV: reading for gist and detail<br>   LA: note-taking<br>   Wo: relationships<br>2) Wo: relationships<br>   LA: asking questions/making a questionnaire<br>3) LA: note-taking<br>   T: collecting arguments<br>   T: writing a comment<br>4) Wo: 'love' idioms<br>   T: Translating idioms into German |
| | **Bewertung:** Aufgabe 1: Zur Überprüfung des Leseverständnisses ergänzen S die vorbereitete Tabelle. Für die korrekte Angabe des Berufes wird je 1 Punkt vergeben. Die *statements* der Personen zum Thema *marriage* sollten je nach Umfang mit 2 oder mehr Punkten bewertet werden. Zusatzpunkte sollten vergeben werden für von der Textvorlage sprachlich gelöste Formulierungen. Aufgabe 2: Da den S durch die Angabe möglicher Themen und die Beispiele Hilfen gegeben werden, dürfte die Bewältigung der Aufgabe auch für schwächere S möglich sein. Zu bewerten sind neben der Originalität der *statements* die Sprachrichtigkeit und das Ausdrucksvermögen sowie die geforderte Struktur, die eine *true/false* Zuordnung möglich macht. Auch die Verwendung situations- und adressatengerechten Vokabulars[3] sollte besondere Berücksichtigung bei der Bewertung finden. Aufgabe 3 verlangt von S – in zwei Teilschritten – das Verfassen eines ausführlichen Kommentars. In schwachen Lerngruppen kann das Sammeln der Vor- und Nachteile gesondert bewertet werden, dabei sind vor allem die Originalität der Argumente, der Umfang und die sprachliche Darstellung zu bewerten. In leistungsstarken Lerngruppen sollte das Anfertigen einer Pro-Kontra-Liste nur als Unterstützung für die Ausformulierung gelten und deshalb nicht getrennt gewertet werden. Hier wird der Text in seiner Gesamtheit betrachtet: Die Formulierung der eigenen Meinung, Vor- und Nachteile, Gründe und Beispiele. Die Ausführlichkeit, Differenziertheit und Originalität des *comments* ergeben die inhaltliche Note. Sprachlich werden Ausdrucksvermögen, Sprachrichtigkeit und die Verknüpfung der einzelnen Textteile berücksichtigt. Sprach- und Inhaltsnote sollten zu je 50% in die Bewertung eingehen. Aufgabe 4: Bei dieser Aufgabe zur Wortschatzerweiterung und -differenzierung (vgl. SB S. 65, Aufg. 1) sollten pro korrektem Übersetzungsvorschlag 1–2 Punkte vergeben werden. | | |
| 3. | Fly me into space | 1) halboffen<br><br>2a) halboffen<br><br>2b) offen<br>3) offen<br>4) offen | 1) LA: understanding a picture story<br>   T: writing a story/describing the pictures<br>2a) Wo/Wi: formal/informal English<br>    T: rewriting informal sentences<br>2b) T: giving polite answers<br>3) T: writing a comment/giving one's opinion<br>4) T: giving one's opinion |
| | **Bewertung:** Aufgabe 1: Auf der Inhaltsebene wird hier die logische Verknüpfung der Geschehnisse und die Ausgestaltung der inhaltlichen Details bewertet. Hinsichtlich der Sprache sollten Sprachrichtigkeit und die Verwendung angemessenen Vokabulars bewertet werden. Sprache und Inhalt gehen zu gleichen Teilen in die Endnote ein. Aufgabe 2 bezieht sich auf die in der *Topic* gübten Kommunikationsregeln *(Communicating successfully* – SB S. 66). Bei der Teilaufgabe a) wird die sprachliche Leistung bewertet. Entscheidend ist, ob die Formulierungen der S auch wirklich in höflichem Englisch geschrieben sind. Pro *statement* sollten 2 Punkte vergeben werden (Punktabzug bei Mängeln bzgl. Sprachrichtigkeit). Teilaufgabe b) erfordert inhaltlich die adäquate Reaktion der Gesprächspartner und sprachlich erneut die Formulierung in höflichem Englisch. Hier werden 2–3 Punkte je *statement* gegeben. Aufgabe 3: Die Ausführlichkeit und Differenziertheit der Begründungen sollte bei der Bewertung des Inhalts im Mittelpunkt stehen. Die sprachliche Note ergibt sich aus der Sprachrichtigkeit und der Verwendung strukturierenden Vokabulars. Die Inhalts- und Sprachnote sollten zu gleichen Teilen in die Bewertung einfließen. Aufgabe 4 löst sich von der Textvorlage und bezieht sich auf mögliche Wünsche und Träume der S. Die Formulierung der eigenen Meinung und der Begründungen in ihrem Umfang ergeben die Inhaltsnote, die Sprachnote setzt sich aus der Sprachrichtigkeit, dem Ausdrucksvermögen und der Strukturierung der einzelnen Textteile zusammen. | | |

# TOPIC 4

| 4. | Three girls out | 1) halboffen<br>2) offen<br>3) offen<br>4) offen | 1) LV: reading for detail<br>    T: paraphrasing the contents<br>2) Wi/Wo: film/books<br>    T: answering questions<br>3) T: giving one's opinion<br>4) T: continuing a dialogue (creative writing) |
|---|---|---|---|

**Bewertung:** In Aufgabe 1 wird das Leseverständnis überprüft. Je korrekter Satzergänzung können 2 Punkte (je 1 Punkt für sprachliche und inhaltliche Richtigkeit) vergeben werden. Aufgabe 2 geht inhaltlich über die Überprüfung des Textverständnisses hinaus. S beantworten mit Hilfe eigener Kenntnisse über Filme und Bücher die Fragen. Bei der Beantwortung sollte inhaltlich vor allem die Differenziertheit und die Ausführlichkeit berücksichtigt werden. Die Sprachnote, die zu gleichen Teilen mit der Inhaltsnote in die Bewertung eingehen sollte, ergibt sich vor allem aus Sprachrichtigkeit und Ausdrucksvermögen. Aufgabe 3: Inhaltlich werden hier die eigene Stellungnahme und Begründung bzgl. des Umfangs und der Differenziertheit bewertet. Die Sprachnote ergibt sich aus Sprachrichtigkeit, Ausdrucksvermögen und Strukturierung der Darstellung. Besondere Bedeutung spielen bzgl. der Sprachrichtigkeit die Formen des Konditionals, die bei der Begründung aufgrund der Fragestellung immer wieder verwendet werden müssen *(Would you have left...?)*. Inhalt und Sprache sollten zu gleichen Teilen in die Bewertung einfließen. Aufgabe 4: Bei dieser kreativen Aufgabe steht eindeutig der inhaltliche Aspekt im Vordergrund der Bewertung. Die Originalität, der Umfang und die Kohärenz des Dialoges werden hier besonders berücksichtigt. Die Sprachnote, die nicht so stark gewichtet werden sollte wie die Inhaltsnote, setzt sich zusammen aus Ausdrucksvermögen, Strukturierung der Darstellung und Sprachrichtigkeit. Umgangssprachliche Wendungen und Kurzformen sind hier nicht nur erlaubt sonderen erforderlich und sollten positiv in die Bewertung aufgenommen werden.

| 5. | After the party | 1) geschlossen<br>2) offen<br>3) offen | 1) HV: reading for gist and detail<br>2) T: comparing different characters/giving one's opinion<br>3) Gr: making adjectives with the help of suffixes<br>    T: characterization<br>    T: describing situations |
|---|---|---|---|

**Bewertung:** Bei der ersten Aufgabe zur Überprüfung des Hörverstehens sollte 1 Punkt pro korrektem *statement* gegeben werden. Aufgabe 2: Bei dieser Stellungnahme werden neben der Formulierung der eigenen Meinung die Begründungen im Mittelpunkt der Bewertung stehen. Der Umfang und die Stimmigkeit der Argumentation ergeben die Inhaltsnote. Inhalts- und Sprachnote (ergibt sich aus Sprachrichtigkeit, Verwendung angemessenen Vokabulars und Strukturierung der Darstellung) sollten zu gleichen Teilen in die Bewertung einfließen. Aufgabe 3: Die Aufgabe geht über die reine Hörverstehensleistung hinaus. Vielmehr bilden S zunächst Adjektive, die dann in einem weiteren Schritt der Charakterisierung der Hauptpersonen dienen. In leistungsschwachen Lerngruppen kann für die Bildung der Adjektive eine Vergabe von Punkten vorgesehen werden. Die Beschreibung der einzelnen Charaktere und Situationen wird dann in einem zweiten Schritt bzgl. Umfang der Ausführungen und Sprachrichtigkeit bewertet. Großes Gewicht wird auf die Begründung gelegt, die in besonderem Maße mit in die Inhaltsnote einfließt. In leistungsstarken Lerngruppen kann auf eine Bewertung der Adjektivbildung verzichtet werden. Hier wird lediglich die Beschreibung von Charakteren und Situationen bewertet (s. o.).

# TOPIC 4

## 1 I believe in you!

Martin was a bad boy. He bullied other kids, he was cheeky[1] to his teachers, his head was full of jokes which weren't jokes to the kids he played them on. Martin was hopeless and would leave school without any GCSEs. That was certain.

When, at the end of Year 7, he asked Mrs White if he could change classes and be in her class, she wasn't very pleased. She thought of her nice class and then looked at the boy with his dirty clothes who always smelt as if he needed a bath. When she asked him why he wanted to change he said that she reminded him of his mum. At the end of the school year Mrs White was too busy to explain to the boy that she didn't want him – so she agreed.

But during the summer holidays she tried to find out a bit more about Martin. In Years 1–4 his teachers had given him very good reports[2]: "Martin is a clever child, well-liked by his classmates, does his work neatly[3] and behaves well." His Year 5 teacher had written, "His mother's death has been hard on him. Martin hasn't got many friends and doesn't seem to be interested in lessons. He sometimes sleeps in class." Mrs White called the teacher and found out that Martin's mother had died of cancer[4], and that his father, a dentist[5], didn't show any interest in the boy. So that was Martin's problem: He missed his mum, and his father didn't care.

In Year 8 Martin joined her class. When it was her birthday, the other kids gave her nice presents but Martin gave her a tired-looking bunch[6] of wild flowers. The class started to laugh, but Mrs White stopped them. She cut the flowers to freshen them and put them in a vase on her desk.

After the lesson Martin came up to her and said: "My mum and I used to pick[7] wild flowers and decorate the house with them." From that day on Mrs White made sure that there were always wild flowers in her classroom. One day, when they were alone in the classroom, Mrs White told Martin that she had to go to the dentist and that she was afraid to go. Martin looked at her for a while and then he told her that his father was the best dentist in the world and shouldn't they go together? He would hold her hand – that helped. Mrs White agreed.

"See," Martin said after the visit, "my father is just the best."

"And you are, too, Martin," Mrs White said.

At the end of Year 9 Martin got some GCSEs, but he still wasn't a brilliant student. Mrs White found a message from Martin in her letter-box, telling her that she was the best teacher at school.

After he left school, he started sending her Christmas cards, telling her that he had started and finshed his apprenticeship[8] as a dental technician[9], that he had started studying at university to become a dentist and would she come to celebrate his doctor's degree.

Mrs White went for a long walk and picked a lot of wild flowers. It took her about an hour to arrange them into a beautiful bunch as a present for Martin.

When they met he introduced Mrs White to his wife who was pregnant. "It's going to be a girl," he told her, "and we're going to call her Anna, after you. Thank you for believing in me."

"You got it all wrong," she said, "I needed you, because there was something wrong with my teeth. And now your father isn't working any more, I need a good dentist. I'm just selfish. I know you'll be very careful with me, won't you?"

**1.** Make a time chart of Martin's life. Take the information (school/apprenticeship/university) from the text and use your general knowledge.
You can start like this:

| Years 1–4 | Martin is a brilliant student |
|---|---|
| Year 5 | ... |
| ... | |

**2.** Describe key situations in the relationship between Martin and Mrs White.

**3.** From your own experience or a friend's tell a story in which a teacher helped you or your friend a lot.

**4.** Martin the dentist is looking at his timetable for the following day. This is what he is telling his assistant. Use future progressive or future perfect to complete Martin's sentences.

1. This time tomorrow Mrs White _____ (sit) in the chair.

2. I _____ (look) at her teeth.

3. We _____ (talk) about old times.

4. By the weekend Mrs White _____ (forget) the pain.

5. I _____ (invite) her to dinner.

6. And Mrs White _____ (speak) to my father.

7. So she _____ (tell) my father that I'm a brilliant dentist.

[1] **cheeky** – frech; [2] **report** – Zeugnis; [3] **neat** – ordentlich; [4] **cancer** – Krebs; [5] **dentist** – Zahnarzt; [6] **bunch** – Strauß; [7] **to pick** – pflücken; [8] **apprenticeship** – Lehre; [9] **dental technician** – Zahntechniker

# TOPIC 4

## 2 The key to a happy marriage

Would Romeo and Juliet have made a happy couple? Would their marriage have been a success?
Well, they wasted a lot of time talking about their relationship. Instead they should have each taken a pencil and done Professor Jerry Collins' questionnaire to find out if they had any chance of a happy marriage or whether they should split up before their lives came to a tragic end.

Jerry Collins, professor of marriage and family studies at Durham University, UK, explained that if couples did his questionnaire, the number of divorces and unhappy marriages could go down a lot.

In the questionnaire they have to put true or false next to statements on topics that range[1] from money, hobbies and expressing[2] feelings to children, problems etc. If the couples' answers do not match at all, they should not get married.

Professor Collins' research[3] is based on 15 years' experience and studies of more than 200 couples. "Love simply isn't enough," he explained yesterday. "You shouldn't marry the person you love if the results of the questionnaire differ radically." And he says that couples should not marry if they are under 24, if they haven't known each other for more than two years, if they don't agree about children, or if they hate each other's hobbies.

Betty French, a marriage guidance counsellor[4], said the questionnaire was like giving a list of possible accidents to a person who has just got his or her driving licence. "No one knows if a marriage will be a success," she said, "because people are changing all the time. It is situations you get thrown into and how you deal with them that make a successful or unsuccessful marriage. Life will teach you if you can go on living together, not a questionnaire." She advises couples to take part in courses to prepare them for a life together.

In Britain 250,000 couples get married every year and about 100,000 will split up during the first three years of marriage. Deirdre Dawkins, a family lawyer[5], said the questionnaire would not put her out of business. "The divorce rate is high, because people get married for all sorts of reasons: Sometimes they want children, or good sex, or even to feel protected and not have to work every day."

1. *Read the text, make a grid like this and fill it in.*

| name | profession[6] | important statements about marriage |
|---|---|---|
| Jerry Collins | | |
| Betty French | | |
| Deidre Dawkins | | |

2. *Make a questionnaire with five statements about marriage and relationships. People who do the questionnaire have to put true or false next to the statements. Look at the box for ideas.*
   Examples: money: The wife should not earn more money than the husband.
   problems: If there are problems, time will solve them.

| friends | money | children | babies | hobbies | problems | education | feelings | relatives | arguments |

3. Would you do a questionnaire to see if you should marry someone? *Collect pros and cons in a list first, then decide if you would or would not. Give reasons and examples.*

4. <u>Here are some expressions with 'love'.</u> *What do you think they mean in German?*
   Jerry Collins has sent his questionnaire to a cousin who wants to get married.

Dear Jerry,
Thank you for the questionnaire, from Victoria, too. She <u>loves doing</u> questionnaires and <u>sends</u> you her <u>love</u>. <u>We'd love to visit you</u> and bring it back ourselves, but we're so busy with the wedding and everything.
Brenda has helped us a lot. We couldn't get a hotel for the reception <u>for love nor money</u>. But she found one and organized the church for us! She says it's just her <u>love of helping</u> others but we must give her something.
We can't expect her to do it <u>for love</u>.
I think Brenda has perhaps found <u>the love of her life</u>. Philip is the manager of the hotel. At first there was <u>no love lost</u> between them, but yesterday she came back with a big <u>love bite</u> on her neck. This morning Philip had sent a bunch of red roses to his <u>love</u>!
<u>With our love</u>
George

---

[1] **to range** – umfassen; [2] **to express** – ausdrücken; [3] **research** – Forschung; [4] **marriage guidance counsellor** – Eheberater/in;
[5] **lawyer** – Rechtsanwalt; [6] **profession** – Beruf

# TOPIC 4

## 3 Fly me into space

For her work experience Susan Griffiths from England went to Huntsville, Alabama, where she was trained with 15 other teenagers at the U.S. Space and Rocket Center. She had to do some of the training astronauts do. She said it was hard work but fun. Susan was on a team with three American boys. Here are some pictures which tell you what happened to Susan.

**1.** *Look at the pictures. Write sentences to go with each picture to tell the story.*

**2. a)** Part of Susan's training was about communicating successfully. "I made a lot of mistakes" Susan said. "I think I will be more careful about what I say in future."
*Here are some of Susan's 'mistakes'. Put her statements into polite English.*

① "Hey, you've got the wrong button again! I said the green one, didn't I." (picture 1)
② "You promised to check the equipment, Tad. It's all your fault!" (picture 4)
③ "Don't be such wimps! Okay? I'll go next." (picture 5)
④ "Hey, stop holding me so tight! I can hardly breathe any more!" (picture 4)
⑤ "Why are you staring at me like that? I can't find my passport, that's all!" (picture 7)

**b)** *How do Susan's partners react in each case to her polite statements?*

**3.** Team training was one part of Susan's work experience. *Say why it is especially important to work and react as a team when you train to become an astronaut.*

**4.** *Would you like to train as an astronaut for your work experience? Give reasons for your opinion.*

# TOPIC 4

## 4 Three girls out

*Without telling their parents, Clare (14), Sue (15) and Carlene (16) go to a party. They have been invited by Tim (22). When they get to the house, the party has already started. Tim's sister, Val, opens the door.*

|   |   |
|---|---|
| Val: | Tim, you forgot to tell us that you'd invited the kindergarten as well! |
| Tim: | *(to Clare, Sue and Carlene)* Don't take any notice of her, girls, she's always like that. |
| Kevin: | Oh, hello, new faces! But aren't they – don't get me wrong, Tim – a bit on the young side? |
| Clare: | *(whispering)* Let's get out of here! |
| 5 Sue: | *(whispering)* Why? |
| Carlene: | You mean leave? |
| Sue: | Ssh! |
| Kevin: | *(handing them drinks)* Here are some drinks for the three of you. |
| Clare: | What's in it? |
| 10 Kevin: | Meet my friend, Jake. He'll tell you. *(Goes away)* |
| Jake: | Oh, er … it's … um … just a kind of fruit juice. It's nice. Try it, okay? |
| Clare: | I still don't know what it is. |
| Jake: | Don't you worry, love. Now, you smoke, don't you? Have one of mine. *(Sue takes a joint from Jake, smokes it, then passes it on to Carlene.)* |
| 15 Val: | *(coming up to them)* Hey, Jake, don't you think your little girlfriends are a bit young for those drinks and your special cigarettes? |
| Jake: | You're spoiling my evening, Val, and your brother's business. It's never too early to start – having fun, I mean. Now tell me, what's your name, love? |
| Clare: | I'm Clare, and these are my friends Sue and Carlene. |
| 20 Tim: | *(handing a glass to Sue)* Here is some more juice for you! |
| Sue: | But I haven't finished my first drink yet. Sorry, but I feel a bit dizzy[1]. |
| Tim: | Don't worry. You'll feel great in a few minutes, believe me. I know what I'm talking about. |
| Clare: | *(taking the joint from Carlene)* This cigarette looks funny. I've never seen one like it before. *(She takes a drag[2] and coughs.)* |
| 25 Jake: | *(takes it away from her, laughing)* One deep drag only, little princess, that's enough for the first time. Did Tim tell you about the band I'm in? We've got this great lead singer, she … |
| Carlene: | Where's the toilet, please? I'm going to be sick[3] in a minute. |
| Jake: | Tim! Tim! One of your little girlies needs the toilet. Get Val to help her. |

30 *(Loud knocking on the front door)*

|   |   |
|---|---|
| Policeman: | Open up! It's the police! |
| Tim: | *(whispering)* Quick, everyone. Open the windows. Hide everything! *(He goes to the front door and opens it.)* |
| Policeman: | Right, everyone stay where they are with their hands behind their backs! We're going to search this place. Here is the search warrant[4]! |
| 35 Tim: | *(to all the others)* Don't say anything. We've got the right not to say anything. |
| Policewoman 1: | Whose party is this? |
| Tim: | Val's and mine. Our parents are on holiday. *(Carlene moves towards the toilet.)* |
| 40 Policewoman 2: | *(grabbing Carlene's arm)* Come on, little girl, stay with me for a while! |
| Carlene: | Sorry, but I've got to go to the toilet! |
| Policewoman 1: | *(moving round the room)* Well, well, well, this is very interesting: speed, ecstasy, hash – and what have we got here? A little cocaine perhaps? |
| Policeman: | All right! Let's move! All of you! We're taking you all down to the police station! |
| 45 Carlene: | Can't I go to the toilet first? |
| Policewoman 2: | Sorry! Hard luck. We'll be at the police station in five minutes. You can go there! |

---

[1] **dizzy** – schwindelig; [2] **drag** – Zug; [3] **to be sick** – sich übergeben; [4] **search warrant** – Durchsuchungsbefehl

# TOPIC 4

**1.** *Read the text carefully then finish the sentences to get a storyline.*

1. The party is given by _____

   when their parents _____

2. Val and Kevin think Sue, Clare and Carlene _____

3. The girls are offered a drink, but _____

4. In the first part of the text Jake says something that suggests that Tim _____

5. Jake makes the three girls _____

6. When Carlene feels sick and needs a toilet _____

7. Although Tim tries to make his friends hide everything, the police _____

8. The policewoman doesn't allow _____

9. All the party guests _____

10. The policewoman tells Carlene that _____

**2.** Why? Why? Why?
*This scene has got a lot of open questions. Try to answer them by using your knowledge from films or books.*
① Why didn't Carlene, Clare and Sue tell their parents where they were going?
② Why did Tim invite the girls to the party?
③ Why doesn't Kevin ask the three girls what they want to drink?
④ When Clare says, "Let's get out of here!" why don't the girls leave?
⑤ Why does Jake start telling Clare about his band?
⑥ Why do the police search the house?
⑦ Why is the whole group taken to the police station?
⑧ Why doesn't the police woman allow Carlene to go to the toilet?

**3.** *Imagine you were one of the girls. Would you have left when Clare said, "Let's get out of here!"? Give reasons for your answer.*

**4.** *The girls have arrived at the police station. Continue the dialogue between the girls and the police officers.*

## 5 After the party

**1.** *Listen to the three mums, then mark the following statements right or wrong.*

| Clare's mum | Sue's mum | Carlene's mum |
|---|---|---|
| – is hurt because her daughter didn't tell her about the party. ____ | – says that she knew Tim's parents. ____ | – is not really interested in her daughter's problems. ____ |
| – wants to treat¹ her daughter as an adult. ____ | – will tell Sue's teachers about the party. ____ | – tells Carlene that she has got a terrible stomach ache. ____ |
| – wants to punish² Clare. ____ | – is angry because Sue only seems to think of herself. ____ | – asks Carlene to talk to somebody else. ____ |

**2.** *Compare the three mums. Who do you like best and why?*

**3.** *Add suffixes to the following words to make adjectives. Then describe a situation or a character from the text. Give reasons for your description.*
*Example:* Clare's mum is lovable because she understands her daughter.

| love | speech | heart | help | hate | wonder | rely | fashion | | -less | -able | -full |

---
¹ **to treat** – behandeln; ² **to punish** – bestrafen

© Ernst Klett Verlag GmbH, Stuttgart 2001.

# TOPIC 5

| Nr. | Aufgabe/Klassenarbeit | Aufgabenform | Lernschwerpunkte |
|---|---|---|---|
| 1. | Just south of the border | 1) geschlossen | 1) LV: reading for detail<br>LA: comparing a text and a picture |
| | | 2) halboffen | 2) LV: reading for detail<br>LA: note-taking/collecting information |
| | | 3) offen | 3) T: describing feelings; commenting on the end of a story |
| | | 4) offen | 4) Wo: dreams and illusions<br>T: finding reasons/giving explanations |
| | | 5) offen | 5) T: analyzing a situation/giving explanations from one's own experience |
| | | 6a) geschlossen | 6a) Gr: finding noun endings |
| | | 6b) geschlossen | 6b) Wo: nouns<br>LA: using a dictionary |

**Bewertung:** Aufgabe 1: Bei dieser Aufgabe kommt es darauf an, Details zu verstehen und im Bild-Text-Vergleich die Fehler zu korrigieren. Pro gefundenem Detail werden 2 Punkte vergeben (Inhalt und Sprache). Aufgabe 2: Auch diese Aufgabe überprüft das Textverständnis im Detail. Je genanntem Teilaspekt können 1–2 Punkte vergeben werden. Aufgabe 3: Bei dieser Aufgabe müssen S sich in die Hauptfiguren der Geschichte hinein versetzen und deren Gefühle begründen. Inhaltlich wird die Ausführlichkeit, Prägnanz und Kohärenz der Darstellung bewertet. Die Sprachnote, die sich aus Sprachrichtigkeit, Verwendung adäquaten Vokabulars und Strukturierung der Darstellung ergibt, sollte zu gleichen Teilen wie die Inhaltsnote in die Bewertung eingehen. Aufgabe 4 knüpft an SB S. 85 an. Sie geht über die Textarbeit hinaus und fordert S zu Spekulationen bzgl. der Zukunft des Protagonisten auf. Ausführlichkeit und Differenziertheit bilden die Grundlagen der Inhaltsnote – Sprachrichtigkeit und Ausdrucksvermögen die der Sprachnote. Sprach- und Inhaltsnote sollten jeweils zu 50% in die Endnote einfließen. Aufgabe 5 transferiert die Thematik des Textes in die Lebenswelt der S. Auf ihren eigenen Erfahrungen und Kenntnissen basierend, bearbeiten sie diese Aufgabe. Die Bewertung lehnt sich an die in Aufgabe 4 zugrunde gelegten Maßstäbe an. Die Aufgaben 6a) und b) dienen der Wortschatzdifferenzierung und -erweiterung. Sie dürften auch leistungsschwächeren S keine Schwierigkeiten bereiten. Zur Erledigung von Aufgabenteil a) sollte S ein Wörterbuch zur Verfügung stehen, da nicht alle zu bildenden Begriffe bekannt sind. Je gebildetem Nomen wird 1 Punkt vergeben. In Aufgabenteil b) bringen S die neu gebildeten Begriffe in einen Kontext. Für jeden korrekt eingesetzen Begriff können max. 2 Punkte vergeben werden.

| 2. | Above the clouds | 1a) halboffen | 1a) LV: reading for detail<br>LA: note-taking |
|---|---|---|---|
| | | 1b) offen | 1b) Wo: jobs/work<br>T: asking questions about a job |
| | | 2) offen | 2) T: writing a comment/giving one's opinion |
| | | 3a) offen | 3a) LA: starting a conversation |
| | | 3b) offen | 3b) LA: continuing a conversation (creative writing) |
| | | 3c) geschlossen | 3c) LA: ending a conversation |

**Bewertung:** Aufgabe 1: Aufgabenteil a) überprüft das Textverständnis. Je eingetragenem Aspekt können 2 Punkte vergeben werden (je 1 Punkt für Inhalt und Sprache). Im Aufgabenteil b) können für die korrekte Formulierung von Fragen Punkte vergeben werden. Die sprachliche Leistung steht bei dieser Aufgabe im Mittelpunkt – sowohl die Form der Fragestellung als auch die Verwendung situationsgerechten Vokabulars werden neben der Sprachrichtigkeit bewertet. Aufgabe 2: Das Nennen der eigenen Meinung und das Formulieren entsprechender Begründungen stehen bei dieser Aufgabe im Vordergrund. In leistungsschwachen Lerngruppen kann die Gewichtung der Sprachnote (Sprachrichtigkeit/Ausdrucksvermögen) zugunsten der Inhaltsnote reduziert werden (z. B. Inhalt 70%/Sprache 30%). Aufgabe 3: Das Thema der *Strategy pages* der *Topic (Conversation* – SB S. 81/82) wird an dieser Stelle aufgegriffen. Aufgabenteil a) führt mit einer recht einfachen Aufgabe auch für leistungsschwache S in die Thematik ein. Teil b) stellt den Hauptteil der zu bewältigenden Leistung dar: S schreiben einen Dialog selbst. Hier sollte die inhaltliche Leistung (Originalität/Umfang) im Vordergrund stehen, um die Kreativität und Fantasie der S zu fördern (und sie nicht mit einer schlechten Note im Bereich Sprache zu demotivieren). Teil c) fordert von S die Entscheidung bzgl. des Endes einer Konversation, nicht aber eine sprachliche Leistung. Hier sollten 2–3 Punkte dafür gegeben werden, dass S ein höfliches Ende, das eine spätere Wiederaufnahme der Kommunikation ermöglicht, von Aussagen, die das Gespräch abrupt beenden ohne dass eine spätere Weiterführung gewünscht wäre, unterscheiden.

| 3. | Why didn't I get the job? | 1) halboffen | 1) HV: listening for detail<br>LA: note-taking |
|---|---|---|---|
| | | 2) geschlossen | 2) HV: listening for detail |
| | | 3) offen | 3) LA: giving advice |

**Bewertung:** Die Aufgaben 1 und 2 überprüfen das Hörverständnis. Wahlweise können in einer Klassenarbeit nur eine oder beide Aufgaben eingesetzt werden. Aufgabe 1 ist wesentlich umfangreicher als Aufgabe 2 und erfordert differenziertes Hörverständnis. Bei Aufgabe 2 genügt es z. T. den Personen entsprechende Stichwörter zuzuordnen. In Aufgabe 1 können je nach Umfang und Qualität der Eintragung Punkte gegeben werden (für *age/marital status/children* genügt 1 Punkt, für die weiteren Informationen sollten mehr Punkte gegeben werden). Aufgabe 2: Diese Aufgabe überprüft das Textverständnis auf einfachem Niveau. Sie dürfte auch leistungsschwächeren S keine Schwierigkeiten bereiten, da schon das Heraushören von *key words* (z. B. 2. *felt sick* ...) zur Lösung führen kann. Je korrekter Eintragung wird 1 Punkt vergeben. Aufgabe 3: Die inhaltliche Bewertung ergibt sich aus der Anzahl und Originalität der Ratschläge. Sprachrichtigkeit, Ausdrucksvermögen und Stil der Darstellung ergeben die sprachliche Bewertung. Beide Bereiche sollten zu gleichen Anteilen in die Bewertung einfließen.

| 4. | The mobile office | 1) geschlossen | 1) LV: reading for detail<br>Wo: work<br>LA: linking headings to parts of the text |
| --- | --- | --- | --- |
| | | 2a) geschlossen<br>2b) offen | 2a)–b) LA: note-taking<br>T: collecting arguments |
| | | 3a) halboffen | 3a) T: describing a picture |
| | | 3b) offen | 3b) T: writing a comment/giving reasons for one's opinion |
| | | 4) geschlossen | 4) Gr: uncountable nouns |

**Bewertung:** Aufgabe 1 überprüft das Leseverständnis. Je korrekter Zuordnung können 1–2 Punkte vergeben werden. Aufgabe 2: Aufgabenteil a) erfordert die intensive Auseinandersetzung mit der Textvorlage. Je gefundenem Argument können 2 Punkte gegeben werden (je 1 Punkt für Inhalt und Sprache). Besonders positiv sollte bewertet werden, wenn S sich sprachlich von der Textvorlage lösen. Da der überwiegende Teil des Textes die Vorteile des *mobile office* hervorhebt, fordert diese Aufgabe von den S z. T. auch ‚zwischen den Zeilen' zu lesen – Vorteile für die Arbeitgeber sind nicht unbedingt auch Vorteile für die Arbeitnehmer. Sollte dieser Aspekt von S erkannt und benannt werden, sollte dies auf jeden Fall sehr positiv bewertet werden. Sofern S eine tabellarische Darstellung wählen, können je Aspekt 2 Punkte (je 1 Punkt für Inhalt und Sprache) gegeben werden. Verfassen S einen zusammenhängenden Text, bietet es sich an, Ausführlichkeit und Qualität der Darstellung inhaltlich zu bewerten. Sprachrichtigkeit, Ausdrucksvermögen und die Strukturierung der Darstellung ergeben dann die Sprachnote. Aufgabe 3: Umfang und Prägnanz der Darstellung (Verwendung adäquaten Vokabulars) ergeben neben der Sprachrichtigkeit die Bewertungsgrundlage für Aufgabenteil a). In Aufgabenteil b) wird für die Bewertung die Nennung der eigenen Meinung und die Ausführlichkeit und Qualität der Begründungen berücksichtigt. Die Sprachnote (Sprachrichtigkeit, Ausdrucksvermögen, Strukturierung) und die Inhaltsnote stellen jeweils 50% der Endnote dar. Aufgabe 4: Hier wird ein zentrales Thema des *language module* der *Topic (Avoiding mistakes with nouns* – SB S. 83) aufgegriffen. Je korrekt genanntem Nomen werden inklusive der entsprechenden Übersetzung 2–3 Punkte vergeben.

# TOPIC 5

## 1 Just south of the border[1]

I met Juan in that little border village in Mexico.
When I first saw him, Juan, about 15 years old, was standing at the edge of the market – authentic, tourists would say, unhealthy and dirty to be honest. Juan was standing well away from the stalls, looking at the things on offer – exotic fruit, vegetables I had never seen in my life before, meat with millions of flies all over it, things that would give Europeans a lot of problems if not peeled[2] or well cooked.

Juan was not begging, he didn't want to annoy[3] anybody. He was in rags[4], his face was dirty, and there was this empty expression of continuous hunger and hopelessness on his face.

A little boy, also in rags, went up to him, put his dirty hand into Juan's and tried to make him move. "Let's go," his eyes said, "it's no good." But Juan didn't move. He ignored the child. Suddenly he went up to one of the stalls and the owner gave him a big bone with bits of meat on it – not even interesting for a dog back home in Europe. Juan smiled, thanked the stall-owner and went back to the little boy, waiting, looking at all the food, the bone in a plastic bag hanging from one of his hands.

Then he moved again, to a different stall, where he was given a few rotten potatoes and some carrots which no other customer would buy. Juan smiled and whistled for his little brother, who came up to him with a smile. The two walked away, the little boy skipping and happy, holding Juan's hand.

I had been so busy watching that it was only after they had left that I realized that these two kids were happy because they had food – not enough, of course, but enough to get through the day.

I couldn't forget Juan's face, so I went to the market again the next day. Same scene, same situation. I offered Juan money, he wouldn't take it. "Story," I said in my broken Spanish.. "I'd like to buy your story," and I put money in his hand. He looked at me and I could see what he was thinking: foreigner – rich – money. I was not rich, but this kid thought I was a millionaire. "Give me your story," I said again, "for money." And I handed him a $10 note. "Comprende español?" he asked me, "Do you understand Spanish?" And then he started talking: His father had left the family three years before. He had crossed the border into the U.S.A. Illegally, of course. He had sent money home during the first three months, but since then they had not heard from him. Three of Juan's brothers and sisters had died during that time, because his mother couldn't pay the doctor or buy any medicine. "She used to work," he told me, "but now she is ill, too." Then Juan smiled. "Maybe I'll go to the U.S.A., too," he said. "It's a rich country, and maybe I'll find my father, if I don't get caught by the American border police."

The following day Juan was not in the market place. His little brother was standing at Juan's usual place. When I asked where his brother was, he shrugged[5] and pointed in the direction of the American border. Then tears filled his eyes and he ran away. I felt guilty, terribly guilty.

**1.** *Look at the picture and the text. There are nine mistakes. Mark them and write down what is wrong. You may use the words in the text.*

[1] **border** – Grenze; [2] **to peel** – schälen; [3] **to annoy** – belästigen; [4] **rag** – Stofffetzen; [5] **to shrug** – mit den Schultern zucken

# TOPIC 5

2. *Read the text then collect in a grid what you get to know about Juan and his family.*

| Juan | father | mother | brothers and sisters |
|------|--------|--------|----------------------|
|      |        |        |                      |

3. The last two sentences of the story are about feelings. *Now you have read the text, say why Juan's brother and the narrator feel the way they do.*

4. *Give reasons why Juan runs away. Mention his hopes and his illusions about the U.S.A.*

5. *Imagine the situation of a family like Juan's in Germany. What would be the same, what would be different?*

6. **a)** *With the help of a dictionary find typical noun endings to the following words from the text.*

| pay       |   |
|-----------|---|
| move      |   |
| happy     |   |
| ill       |   |
| different |   |
| ignore    |   |
| authentic |   |
| illegal   |   |
| beg       |   |
| realize   |   |

**b)** *Look at the following sentences and find the missing nouns. Your list from a) can help you, if not, use your dictionary.*

1. The market was dirty and unhealthy – too much _____ for most Europeans.

2. Juan did not beg for money, he wasn't a _____.

3. He did not move much and when he did, his _____ were slow.

4. The two boys' _____ could be seen. They smiled because they had enough food for the day.

5. The stall owners' _____ for their presents was Juan's smile. They knew he had no money.

6. The narrator did not know much about Juan's situation. Her _____ made her give him money.

7. The _____ between the U.S.A. and Mexico is that the U.S.A. is a rich and Mexico is a poor country.

8. Immigration is almost impossible for Mexicans but many go over the border and live in _____ in the United States.

9. Juan's mother suffered from a bad _____, she could not work any more.

10. Juan had gone over the border to the U.S.A. The _____ of this made the narrator feel guilty.

© Ernst Klett Verlag GmbH, Stuttgart 2001.

# TOPIC 5

## 2 Above the clouds

### Cabin Crew ✈

*Meet new people and make new friends* from Miami to Manhattan, California to the Caribbean as a member of **Virgin Atlantic Cabin Crew**.

Because with stopovers of up to five days at a time, you'll have time to do much more than simply visit the many exciting places we fly to. As exciting as it all sounds, this isn't a job that just anyone could do. As a **flight attendant**[1] with us you'll need energy, initiative, personality and enthusiasm to act as entertainer, diplomat and safety officer during a 13-hour flight. You'll also need to be aged 19–30, be at least 5'2" tall, have a good standard of education and hold an EU passport.

*People this special aren't easy to find,* so we're searching for them all over the country. And we'll be interviewing in your area soon. If you're successful, we won't just offer you the chance to see the world. Based in London you'll **earn good money**, **get free flights** and, after a certain time, **pension** and **private medical insurance**[2]. On top of all this, you'll enjoy long-term career chances – both in the air and on the ground – accelerated[3] by our own continued expansion.

☎ **Call our 24-hour recruitment**[4] **hotline now on 01483 461461**

1. a) *List what Virgin Atlantic offers and what they expect their flight attendants to be like and to be able to do.*

| Virgin Atlantic offers … | Virgin Atlantic expects … |
|---|---|
| | |
| | |
| | |
| | |
| | |

b) *Imagine you want to apply for the job. Write down six questions you would like to ask the Virgin Atlantic people in an interview.*

2. *Would you like to become a member of Virgin Atlantic Cabin Crew? Say why/why not.*

3. *Imagine you are a flight attendant during a 13-hour flight. There is an old lady who is worried about the flight.*
   a) *What can you talk about to start a conversation on a 'safe' topic?*

---

[1] **flight attendant** – Flugbegleiter/in; [2] **medical insurance** – Krankenversicherung; [3] **accelerated** – beschleunigt; [4] **recruitment** – Anwerbung

**TOPIC 5**

**b)** *Continue the following dialogue between the member of the cabin crew and the old lady but don't write an ending. You can start like this:*
Flight attendant: May I ask you what book you are reading?
Old lady: Oh, it's only ...

**c)** *How could the flight attendant end this conversation? Keep in mind he/she wants to look after the old lady. Tick (✓) the best endings.*

Flight attendant:   1. Sorry, but I've got to go now, dinner will be served in a minute. ☐
2. I'll be free after dinner, I'll come back then. You must tell me all about ... ☐
3. You must tell me a bit about ... I'll be with you in about half an hour. Okay? ☐
4. I think I'd better move on, there are other passengers to look after. ☐
5. Well, everyone wants to sleep now. Could you put out your light. ☐

## 3 Why didn't I get the job?

**1.** *Listen to the three applicants for a job as a flight attendant[1]. Then fill in the interviewer's grid.*

| name | Lisa Hopkins | Helen Baxter | Neil Jenkins |
|---|---|---|---|
| age | | | |
| marital status[1] | | | |
| children | | | |
| education | | | |
| suitable/not suitable because ... | | | |

**2.** *Read the following questions which were asked during the three interviews and find out who was asked what.*

| | |
|---|---|
| 1. What would you do with injured people after an accident when suddenly a car starts to burn? | |
| 2. Imagine there was a mother who felt sick on a flight. What would you do with her two children aged two and four? | |
| 3. Can you tell us the difference between the Times and the Sun? | |
| 4. What would you do if you saw two teenagers fighting with knives? | |
| 5. Do you always wear your safety belt when you drive a car? | |
| 6. What would you do if you were very tired but there was still work to do? | |

**3.** *Imagine these three people want to apply for a job with another airline. Give them advice how to react the next time.*

---
[1] **flight attendant** – Flugbegleiter/in; [2] **marital status** – Familienstand

# TOPIC 5

## 4 The mobile office

### The office of the future

**You want to save money. You want to save time.
Time is money.**

Why not save money by closing down most of your offices and letting your staff work from home – or
5   wherever[1] they are? No more money for rent[2], electricity, office furniture and expensive heating. No more staff wasting time and your money by chatting, drinking tea or eating lunch. Now 'Mobile Office' technologies mean your staff can stay fully networked, wherever they are.

10   And your staff will get all the information exactly the moment they need it. Up to now your staff got it in the office, at their desks. Desks are no longer necessary, because access[3] to information, communications and transactions is now possible not just at the workplace.
15   Wherever your staff are – in an airport lounge or at a customer's office, on the road, at home or even in another country – they will be fully functioning, fully networked and fully integrated members of your organization.

The new 'Mobile Office' concept helps to get
20   information to your staff even while they are meeting customers. At the same time they can get all the help and advice they need. The concept is to give up the idea of work as a place where people go, and to present work as an activity which can be done everywhere.

25   The new 'Mobile Air Service' gives staff the chance to receive and make calls on a plane. Special phones are installed in each passenger's seat. Phone calls are made via[4] satellite. British Airways, Virgin Atlantic, Swiss Air, Lufthansa etc. will be equipped with 'Mobile Air
30   Service' during the coming months.

Erica Emerson works via 'Mobile Office' technologies from home: "It has given me such freedom to be able to work from home. As a mother of three children and with a husband working full time, I normally would have no chance of a job. Instead I can stay at home and 35 go on working for the firm that I started with six years ago. If I had actually got to go out to work, I would have to spend all the money I earned paying for someone to look after the kids and do the housework.

Peter Benson has been working with 'Mobile Office' 40 technologies for six months: "It's great to get all the information you need wherever you are. I enjoy being on the move all the time, and it's even nicer to be able to work during boring train or plane trips. So I can save time for myself and my family. I do miss my colleagues 45 in the office sometimes, but they are 'Mobile' as well and I can always chat with them via e-mail."

---

**1.** *Which heading goes with which paragraph in the text?*

1. The workplace at home – *paragraph* _____

2. Getting information everywhere _____

3. Save office costs _____

4. For and against 'the mobile office' _____

5. New concept of work _____

6. Communication in the air _____

**2. a)** *Make a list of the advantages of Mobile Office technologies mentioned in the text.*
   **b)** *Look at your list and read the text again. Then find dangers and disadvantages of Mobile Office technologies.*

**3.** *Look at the picture that goes with the text.*
   **a)** *What does it show?*
   **b)** *Decide if the picture is a good or a bad illustration for the text. Give reasons for your answer.*

**4.** *From the text find five uncountable nouns. Translate them into German, then decide if they are uncountable in German, too.*

---

[1] **wherever** – wo immer; [2] **rent** – Miete; [3] **access** – Zugang; [4] **via** – über

# Lösungen und HV-Texte

## TOPIC 1

### 1  For the excitement

**1. a)** You find out that people in a car were killed by young people and that they killed them by throwing stones (rocks).

**b)** Two women were killed when three American boys threw stones from a bridge near Augsburg.

**2.** *who?* – three teenage boys/two dead women/five injured people/police; *where?* – in Augsburg – pedestrian bridge over Ulm-Munich highway; *when?* – the Sunday before February 20th, 2000; *what?* – three boys threw big stones onto moving cars. Several cars were hit, two women died.

**3. Lösungsvorschlag:**
The headline shows that teenagers killed. Young people involved in <u>crime</u> always attract the reader's interest.
At the beginning of the text the author shows that he is on the scene where the accident happened. He mentions the red and white police tape which is used by the police to <u>close off</u> the place where an accident or crime has taken place so that the police can look for any <u>clues</u> or <u>traces</u> of the criminals. Then there is the policeman's statement that he is not allowed to give any information.
Then the author shows that he has taken part in the press conference given by the police and he explains how the police <u>succeeded in</u> arresting the teenage boys.
The last two sentences have got an <u>eye-catcher</u> in the headline of the *Bild* newspaper 'Killer Kids of Augsburg' and they mention that the teenagers could go to prison for more than 10 years.

**4. Lösungsvorschlag:**
The German newspaper *Bild* belongs to the Yellow Press. It's a newspaper which wants to cause sensation rather than give information. With this headline *Bild* appeals to German <u>prejudices</u> against foreigners: The boys are Americans and they are killers. 'American Soldiers' sons' could be positive. Soldiers have got <u>honour</u>, they fight for their country, so their sons should follow their fathers' <u>morals</u>. But the second part of the heading shows the negative aspect. These sons do not follow their fathers but they are killers. Soldiers are killers. American soldiers are not <u>honourable</u>, but fathers and sons do the same: they kill.
This is a headline to <u>provoke</u> an anti-American attitude.
The headline of this article on the other hand gives information. The writer does not mention the kids' nationality. So he puts the stress on the fact that teenagers – their nationality is not important – did something bad – they killed. They killed by throwing stones onto cars. The headline of this article is more neutral, it informs. It doesn't say the stones were thrown with the intention to hit. So maybe the killing happened accidentally.
All in all you can say that the *Bild* headline <u>appeals</u> to the reader's emotions, <u>whereas</u> the headline of this article offers information.

**5. Lösungsvorschlag:**
I think the teenagers were bored and wanted to have some fun. They did not really realize the danger the car drivers were in. But I think they wanted to watch the car drivers' irritation and anger. Maybe they hoped that something would happen – that a car driver would stop his car and shout at them. Then they would have laughed. I can't imagine that it was the boys' intention to kill or to cause an accident.

### 2  Why did they do it?

HV-Text: 37 – 40
*Three teenage boys threw volleyball-sized rocks from a bridge over a four-lane highway near Augsburg. They hit six cars and two women died.*

*Craig:* My name is Craig Smith and I am 14 years old. My father is in the U.S. army here in Germany. We've been here for six months now. There are already plans to move again. Dad has been very busy since we came to Germany so I don't see him a lot. Mom has got her hands full with my little brother and sister, so I try to keep well out of her way.
See, that's how I met Steve and Ian. They taught me how to smoke and took me for rides on their motorcycles. There was always beer and sometimes whiskey and vodka.
What happened that day? I really can't remember very much, because I was drunk. The only thing I remember is a motorcycle ride. We stopped at a bridge and Steve and Ian went off.
I had to keep an eye on their motorcycles. When I heard the crash I knew that something was wrong, but I only realized later what they had done. They came running back and rode off on their motorcycles. They left me behind. I had to walk all the way home.
*Ian:* My name is Ian McDuff and I'm 18. I don't have any brothers or sisters. We have been in Germany for four years now. My father is an officer in the army. I haven't got a job right now.
Life is real boring here, if you want excitement, you have to organise it yourself. We usually ride our motorcycles up and down the highway. You can always frighten the car drivers a bit. But we don't want anything to happen to our motorcycles so we're careful not to cause any accidents.
One day Steve came around with a video. Dead boring! But there was this scene: kids on a bridge – throwing small rocks at cars. And I thought, hey, we could do much better that that! And we did, didn't we?
When I heard the crash and saw all those cars stop, we took off on our motorcycles. Why? That's the whole part of it – you don't get caught.
*Steve:* I'm Steve Browning, 17, and we've been living here for two years now. I've got two brothers and my father works in the army. My mother works at the officers' club and that's where I met Ian. He's a great guy, he can do everything, and he always knows what to do on a boring afternoon.
MY motorcycle? I haven't got one. Ian has got two and he let me have his older one. We often went out on the highway and Ian had this idea about frightening car drivers. Sure, it was dangerous but it sure was a lot of fun. After a while it got boring.
Then I found that video and I just had to show it to Ian. We watched it together over a few beers and Ian said, " Let's try it out." I was going to throw small rocks or sticks onto those cars, but then Ian found these real big rocks and gave them to me. And then I heard the crash. I know that because of what I did two people have died. I'm sorry for those two women, I'm sorry for my parents and for little Craig who has nothing to do with it all. It was us, it really was.

**1.**

| name | age | how he was involved in the incident | what he did after the incident |
|---|---|---|---|
| • Craig Smith | 14 | He kept an eye on the motorcycles. He was drunk. | He walked home. |
| • Ian McDuff | 18 | He had the idea with the stones. He gave the big rocks to Steve. | He went home by motorcycle. |
| • Steve Browning | 17 | He showed the video to Ian. He threw the rocks that killed the two women. | He <u>fled</u> by motorcycle. |

**2. a)** 1. r; 2. w; 3. w; 4. r; 5. w; 6. r; 7. w; 8. r; 9. w; 10. r.
**b)** 2. He was keeping an eye on the two motorcycles.
3. They left Craig behind. He had to walk home.
5. He hasn't got a job right now.
7. He had seen Steve's video.
9. Ian owns two motorcycles.

**3. a)** The three boys were bored. They had watched a video which showed kids on a bridge throwing small stones at cars. Then Ian had the idea of doing the same. So they went to the bridge over the motorway. They wanted to have fun because frightening car drivers with their motorcycles didn't give them a kick any more.

**b)** Craig is not guilty at all. He watched the video but he was drunk, so he didn't know what the two other boys were planning to do and what they actually did. It was his task to keep an eye on their motorcycles. So he was not involved in the crime.
It's hard to decide between Ian and Steve. I think Ian is the most guilty because he is sort of a leader and he handed Steve the rock which actually killed the two women. An intention to kill does not make you guilty. Ian planned the whole thing but he let Steve commit the crime by handing him the big rock. The law probably would say that Steve is the most guilty boy but morally Ian is responsible for what happened.

## 3 The old tunnel

**1.** 1. ... Mick, Amy and the I-narrator.
2. ... go into an old tunnel to smoke and drink.
3. ... there are rats and there is the echo of their footsteps which sounds as if someone is following them.
4. ... Mick marks the two sides of the tunnel with chalk so that they can find their way back.
5. ... she has seen a skeleton sitting on the floor of the tunnel.
6. ... have lost their way out and they hear a strange noise.

**2. a) Lösungsvorschläge:**
The story takes place in an old tunnel. There are a lot of rats. The teenagers shiver because the tunnel is cold and it smells, so at the beginning the kids would hold their noses to show this. The echo plays an important role. Everything they do and say is repeated by the cho. The tunnel must divide so that two ways can be taken by the kids. The torch which the I-narrator has got makes parts of the tunnel visible so that a ghostly atmosphere is created.

**b)** The first key situation is the dividing of the tunnel. Mick marks the sides of the tunnel so they won't get lost. Here the teenagers are in danger, but one of them solves the problem so that they can go on. The finding of the skeleton and the teenagers' reaction on seeing it are the second and the third key situations. To find a skeleton is frightening. The fourth key situation is when they realize they have lost their way and hear the noise they can't explain. The action of the story is carried forward when the teenagers run away. The reader gets curious and wants to know what's going to happen next. The teenagers have lost their way. So there is another problem they have got to solve. Moreover they are endangered by the unexplicable noise which is approaching them. This is a danger they are aware of but the story breaks off before we learn how the teenagers are going to deal with this danger.

**c)** There are three teenagers, one of them tells the story. The I-narrator seems to be a boy. He doesn't mind rats which would frighten most girls. He has got a torch with him, something girls don't usually carry around with them. He is as frightened as the others are, but he isn't scared of ghostly things although the echo worries him as much as the others.
Amy reacts in a way most girls would react when seeing a skeleton. She screams. But she is also the first to notice the skeleton and she says that she wants to leave. She is the one who starts running and the boys follow without thinking.
Mick seems to be a very clever boy. He has the idea of marking the sides of the tunnel and he is the one who stops the running in panic. He states that a skeleton can't do them any harm. It's not a ghost. Nevertheless he follows Amy, too, when she starts running again.

**d)** I think the climax is the reaction of the teenagers when they find the skeleton. When Amy says "I want to go back." (l. 30) you would expect the group to leave the tunnel and inform the police. But the echo frightens them so they blindly run without thinking about the right direction. That's why the danger they are in increases – they lose their way.

**3. Lösungsvorschlag:**
It's exciting to read the story because it's open-ended. You do not know what will happen next.
I don't like it because it gives me nightmares. The setting is ghostly and I would not like to be one of the kids. The skeleton they found would scare me to death.
The most interesting moment is when the kids hear the noise. It's frightening at first, but it could be something that will help the teenagers to find their way out.
The characters are teenagers of my age. I think they are looking for danger and a kick which they get. I like Mick most, because he seems to be clever. Amy is too hysterical and endangers the other two.
I don't understand why they go into a tunnel to smoke and drink. You can do that everywhere.
The story is dramatic because the setting is ghostly and there are so many open questions, e.g. Who is the skeleton? How do they find their way back? Will anybody miss them?
The story doesn't say how it ends. So we don't know if the three kids find their way back out of the tunnel. You don't get information how and why the boy in the tunnel died and if the kids know him. And we don't learn where the strange noise comes from. It could help or endanger the kids.

**4.** 1. were walking, heard;
2. were thinking, took, marked;
3. was watching, yelled;
4. were looking, said;
5. were running, stopped;
6. were listening, heard

## 4 Death in the tunnel

HV-Text: 41 – 42
*In the hills behind Ferndale there are a lot of old mines. The tunnels are dangerous but kids from Ferndale often go there. Wandering around those tunnels gives them a kick. John, Mick and Amy were looking around the tunnels when they found a skeleton. Now they are at the Ferndale Sheriff's to report their find.*

*Sheriff:* Names!
*Mick:* We'd like to report a ...
*Sheriff:* Names!
*Amy:* But you've known us all our lives, Sheriff! Now listen, please! There was this guy sitting there. We wanted to pass and there was this noise ...
*Sheriff:* Don't they teach you in school to answer questions properly any more? Names, I said.
*Mick:* My name is Michael Romero and these are my friends, Amy Klein, and John Davis.
*Sheriff:* Addresses!
*John:* I live at 160 Riverside Walk, Ferndale, and Amy lives ...
*Sheriff:* She can talk herself, can't she? Now Amy, where do you live?
*Amy:* 240 Primrose Drive, Ferndale
*Sheriff:* And you, boy?
*Mick:* 610 Laurel Street, Ferndale.
*Sheriff:* All right, now. What is it all about?
*Mick:* It's about what we saw in the old mining tunnel up in the hills.
*Sheriff:* All the tunnels are closed to the public because they're very dangerous. There are signs all over to stop people from going in.
*Amy:* We know, that's why we came.
*Sheriff:* Oh, is there a sign missing? Did you see someone stealing a sign?
*John:* No, Sheriff, we went into one of the tunnels and ...
*Sheriff:* You went into those tunnels! Didn't your parents tell you how dangerous it is to ...
*Mick:* Sheriff, please listen. We saw a skeleton in there.
*Sheriff:* A skeleton? Oh, yeah! And there were a lot of aliens in there, too, and a lady in white carrying her head under her right arm and ...
*John:* He was wearing tennis shoes – expensive ones – jeans,

and a black leather jacket. The sort of clothes we wear.
*Sheriff:* So you think he was a teenager?
*Amy:* Yes, sir, he was wearing a silver chain with a cross on it and he had a ring with a black stone on his right hand.
*Mick:* Yes, and one of his fingers was missing.
*John:* And then there was this noise …
*Sheriff:* All right, that's it! You've been watching too much X-Files …
*Amy:* No, John is right, it was not only the skeleton that frightened us, but all the rats and the noise …
*Sheriff:* Young lady, I think all of you need a good night's rest. I want you all to come back tomorrow morning at 9 with your parents and then we'll have a nice little talk about wasting people's time and going into dangerous tunnels.

1. The skeleton is wearing trainers, not shoes.
It is wearing jeans, not trousers.
The skeleton has got a black leather jacket.
It is not wearing a cap.
It has got a silver chain with a cross around its neck.
The ring is on the right hand, not on the left hand.

2 a) Correct: 1, 3, 4, 6
b) 2. He interrupts her because he wants to know her name and address.
5. He is astonished/furious/angry.
7. He wants to see them at 9.
8. He says they have been watching too much X-Files.
9. He is angry because he doesn't believe them.

## 5 Basejumper falls 600 feet to death

1. a) 3, 2, 1, 4
b) 1.: the crowd saw Mr Thompson hit the ground at 50 mph – and the man hit the ground at great speed – when the man hit the ground and the film cameras stopped – air cushions and safety sheets which covered the ground – for a minute or so nobody moved. It must have been the shock.
2.: – After a few seconds in free fall his parachute failed to open – He tried to free himself and it seemed as if he would be able to pull the cord of his reserve parachute
– his cord got tangled in the still closed parachute – When this didn't happen I thought it was a trick or something
3.: – hundreds of onlookers – was doing a stunt for an action film – he had to jump from a skyscraper
4th picture: – a member of the American Stunt Man Association – he had been trained … in France and Canada together with a group of 20 other base jumpers – he (John) always tried to persuade young people to do parachuting … because it is much safer –

2. 1. met;
2. have been;
3. have already trained;
4. have just heard;
5. was;
6. went;
7. invited

3. Lösungsvorschlag:
I think most young people are bored with what they do every day. So they look for adventures in which they risk bad injuries or even their lives. If you watch little children you can often see them taking risks. They jump off a swing or stairs. They try to cross a road when they should wait for cars to pass. And they know the danger they are in. Maybe it is in our genes to take risks sometimes. That is one reason why young people do extreme sports like sky surfing, absolute diving or base jumping.

# Topic 2

## 1 The mission

1. 1. A; 2. D; 3. G; 4. C; 5. F; 6. B; 7. E
2. Lösungsvorschlag:
First of all the speaker praises the arson attack which was carried out by a member of the organisation. He points out the very young age of the member who is only 16 years old and has already been very successful. (ll. 2–4)
Then he describes the empy ghetto street which flames have 'cleaned'. (ll 6–7). The speaker does not tell his audience about the black people's feelings when they had to leave their houses. The empty Winfield Road is a promise, because white people may be able to live there. After that the speaker makes his audience look into the future ("And soon all the black ghettos in the U.S.A. will have disappeared" ll. 8–9). Ghetto is a negative word, it is associated with poverty and crime. So the speaker gets the audience's agreement that it is right to destroy ghettos. Then the speaker deepens that vision and leads his listeners' imagination to a time when no black people will be seen in the white people's cities ("… will disappear from our stores, our schools, …" ll. 12–13) This list stresses the fact that at the moment Blacks are everywhere and that in the future they'll be gone.
After that the speaker turns to possible arguments against the aims of the organisation. He does not deal with the arguments themselves but asks his listeners a lot of rhetorical questions ("do you want your daughter or your sister …" ll. 17–19; "Is there anybody in this room … ." ll. 21–27).
The last part of John's speech contains two aspects: first of all he informs his listeners that a new attack is planned ("if this packet is put in the right place … ." ll. 31–32) and then he points out that the organisation is in danger from the press and the police, because there are members who are informers ("… who are spies and traitors" l. 40) By combining these two aspects, the speaker appeals to his listeners as a group who must NOT inform the police or the press, because they are enemies. This shows that the speaker is well aware of the fact that his actions are criminal.
At the end of the speech John seems to look for his listeners' support for his next crime, but in fact his listeners have no choice to refuse their approval (ll. 41–45) They follow him blindly.
By asking three members of the group "to stay behind" (l. 46–47) the speaker refers to earlier in his speech. These three people are going to have "the chance to help with the cleaning and tidying". The rest of the audience would like this chance as well, so they envy these three chosen members and don't realize that they are envying them the chance to commit the next crime.

3. Lösungsvorschlag:
*John:* Well, how did you like the speech?
*Ron:* Smashing, John! It was really great!
*Susan:* I don't know. I'm still a bit frightened about what you said about the police and the press. Imagine if they turned up next time. Or were they here under cover.
*George:* Come on, Susan, what did John actually say? It's his right to speak out against what he doesn't like about our city, isn't it?
*Ron:* … and he didn't say anything that really can be used against us, did he?
*John:* Susan, if you don't want to put that packet in the right place, why don't you tell me?
*Susan:* Please, John, don't get me wrong. I'll give you all the support I can, but I MUST know what is in the parcel, and where we have to put it.
*John:* You know that I work at the hospital, don't you? Now look, yesterday there was this poor black man, and we had to cut off half of his leg …
*Susan:* And you took it? I can't believe it.
*John:* … and I want you to put it …
*Ron:* … in front of the entrance of the ghetto church in Mansfield Drive on Sunday morning before Holy Mass.

# Lösungen und HV-Texte

*John:* Hey, you're a bright kid, aren't you?
*George:* That'll shock the Blacks away. I can already see them running!

4.

| verb | noun | adjective |
|---|---|---|
| to succeed | success | successful |
| to think | thought | thoughtful, thinking |
| to endanger | danger | dangerous, endangered |
| to forget | forgetfulness | forgetful, forgotten |
| to speak | speaker, speech | speechless, speaking |
| to like | like, liking | likeable |
| to thank | thank, thankfulness, thanklessness | thankful, thankless |
| to disappear | disappearance | disappearing |
| to please | pleasure | pleasurable, pleased |
| to explode | explosion, explosive, explosiveness | explosive, exploding |

## 2 Trapped

HV-Text: 43 – 44

Neil has joined a racist organization 'White Up'. John, the leader of the organization, orders Neil to throw a fire bomb at a house in a part of the city where many blacks live. Neil's bomb burns down an empty ghetto house.

*John:* Neil? Did you see the TV news?
*Neil:* Yeah, I did.
*John:* Great job!
*Neil:* Uh ... yeah, but ...
*John:* What's up, Neil?
*Neil:* It was in that report on the news. The blacks are talking about revenge now. I didn't know this was what 'White Up' was all about when I joined. Listen, John, I want out.
*John:* Oh, you do, do you? Well, it's not that simple, Neil. You see, once you've joined 'White Up' you can't leave.
*Neil:* You never told me that. None of the others mentioned it either!
*John:* Well, Neil, just because no one said it, it doesn't mean it isn't true. Now. What are you going to do tonight?
*Neil:* I have a Math assignment. And it's a lot of work. That's what I'm going to do.
*John:* Oh no, that's what you were planning to do, Neil. Now I'm going to tell you what you will actually do. Right?
*Neil:* No, it's not right, John. I'm staying at home and you won't see me again. I'm not coming any more. I'm leaving, and that's it.
*John:* Uh-oh! Just like that? (*Big sigh*) Oh, Neil, you're putting me in a difficult position. You see, I believed in you. Just 16 and already one mission alone. So many members of our organization wanted me to kick you out. They said you were too young, too weak. But did I do it? No! And look at me now. How are you going to repay me? Those people will laugh at me and then they'll look for you. Everywhere. I can't protect you any more. And they will do things to you. ... Things you can't imagine. And there's nothing I can do for you, Neil. And they will find out if you leave, believe me.
*Neil:* Who are these people you are talking about, John? Anyway, I know what I'll do. I'll tell the cops. I'll tell them that I burned down the house. I'll go to jail, but I don't care. And you will be out of it.
*John:* Oh boy! You don't know the cops. Once they've got you they'll get it out of you. All of it. ...
*Neil:* But I won't tell, promise.
*John:* Like you promised to work for us? But listen: Suppose the blacks found out that you threw that bomb!
*Neil:* You can't tell them. They would kill me.
*John:* Sure I can! So listen! We've got something planned for this evening. I want you to be there! 7 o'clock!! See you then!

**1. a)** 1. r; 2. r; 3. n.i.; 4. w; 5. w; 6. r; 7. r; 8. w; 9. w; 10. n. i.
**b)** 4. Neil has got a Math assignment to do. 5. John says 'Now I'm going to tell you what you will actually do...' 8. He says he'll tell the police. 9. He threw a bomb.
**2.** *name:* Neil; *age:* 16; *job:* student (he has to do his Math homework); *name of organization he belongs to:* White up; *what Neil has done:* he has thrown a fire bomb at a house in a black part of town;
*reason why Neil wants to leave:* he is afraid because the black people are talking about revenge;
*what members of the group said against Neil:* he is too young; he is too weak; he must be kicked out;
*John says he'll do this if Neil leaves:* members of the group will find out and punish Neil for leaving (John will probably tell them), he will spread the information among the blacks that Neil was the arson attacker;
*what Neil offers to do:* he offers to tell the police that he committed the arson attack and he will not tell them about the organization;
*what John orders Neil to do at the end of the conversation:* to meet him at 7 o'clock

**3. Lösungsvorschlag:**
If I was in Neil's place, I would phone the police and tell them everything about the organization and that something is planned. Maybe I would get into trouble because of the arson attack, but a good lawyer could help me to find mild judges who would consider my age and the pressure that was put on me. I would admit it was a big mistake to join the organization "White Up", and I could give reasons why I joined it (friends who asked me to go there, etc.). I would offer to tell them the addresses of the meeting places and the names of the members of the organization. I would point out the pressure the leader put on me with his threats. So the police could protect me for a while, but I would be well aware of the danger all the time. Maybe I would change my habits and I would go a different way to school. I would have my mobile phone on me all the time just in case I got into trouble.

**4. Lösungsvorschlag:**
*Neil:* Suppose someone informed the police about your plans for tonight. Suppose someone gave the addresses and the names of your organization to the police. Suppose someone told the police that you planned and committed all those crimes.
*John:* You can't prove anything, and who would believe a criminal?
*Neil:* Sure? Do you remember how you told me about that Black you stabbed to death? Do you remember you told me the police never found the kid's murderer? Do you remember when and where it happened? I do!
*John:* Oh, come on, the police are our enemy. Have you forgotten that?
*Neil:* Sorry, John, but I've got the feeling that YOU are my enemy now. So, leave me alone, and nothing will happen. Okay?
*John:* We'll get you. Just wait and see!
*Neil:* I'll write everything down and put it in a safe place. But if something should happen to me, my family will find it. I not afraid of you any more. Just stay away from me! Bye!

## 3 Bullying in Schools

1. A ... there are a lot of organisations that offer help
B ... the actions against a student happen again and again and are planned.
C ... train teachers and students to recognize the first signs of bullying.
D But students can also get help by law, because some types of bullying – such as threats or physical attacks – are crimes.
E Bullying means that one student or a group of students feels stronger than the student who is bullied.
F ... inform students what to do and where to go if they are bullied.

G What students can do. Students should …
2. Ray: That's not bullying because Ray's classmates punished him for blabbing.
Nicholas: That's bullying. A group of kids have intimidated Nicholas so he didn't go to school any more.
Shirley: That's not bullying, because her classmate has not done anything like it before. Bullying is something that happens more than once.
Sammy: That's bullying. The rumour started three months ago. And spreading gossip is a form of bullying.

## 4 This is school, too

HV-Text: 45 – 46
*Jeremy:* I've already changed schools twice, because I couldn't stand it any more. And now it's started here, too. I first realized that something was wrong when nobody wanted to sit next to me. When the only empty seat was next to me, the other kids fetched a chair from the classroom next door. I'm just an average student, but sometimes our lessons are quite interesting, and I want to know more and I ask questions. Then I hear my classmates saying: "Shut up, Professor!" But I don't want to and I can't stop myself. The teachers seem to be on my classmates' side and tell me to stop. I don't know what's wrong with my questions.
Then my things sort of disappeared: files, books, all sorts of things. At first I thought I'd lost them, but after a day or two they appeared again – dirty and covered with rude words. This had happened at my last school so I could deal with it. The new thing is that the other day I was called to our Head and he told me to keep my hands off the boys from Year 7. At first I didn't know what he was talking about. And when I realized I was so shocked I couldn't say anything.
When I got back to my class I found I'd got a new name: Gay Lord.
*Natalie:* We are really afraid of her, and I can't believe she is still in our class and nothing has happened. She goes around with five other girls from Year 9 to 11. They are a real gang. The teachers know about them. But what can they do?
It started when we were 11 years old, when she made us do her homework. We had to write like her, which was very difficult. Next thing she did, was to collect money – for presents for the teachers she said – but when we wanted to buy a present for our teacher, there wasn't any money left. She had spent it on herself.
Then she forced us to give her our lunch tickets which she sold to older kids or gave to her gang. If we didn't do what she wanted, she waited for us at the bus stop and hit us. I had to go to the doctor twice.
Even the teachers don't know how to deal with her. One teacher tried, but then she told us she had been at his home three or four times – alone. He isn't married. He got really angry, but it didn't stop her.
The strange thing is we are so frightened of her – even the boys – that some of us try to be as friendly to her as we can. The other day three boys were stealing make up for her in a department store when they got caught. I don't know what they told their parents but definitely nothing about the girl.

**1. a)** Jeremy: 2 – 3 – 5; Natalie: 3 – 4 – 6 – 7
**b)** Jeremy
2: They call Jeremy 'Professor' and 'Gay Lord'. 3: The bullies have told the headmaster that Jeremy is interested in the boys in Year 7, which is not true. 5: The bullies hide Jeremy's things: When he finds them later they are dirty and covered with rude words.
Natalie
3: The bully tells stories about her visit to her teacher's home. 4: The bully hits the students who don't do what she wants. 6: The bully makes the girls do her homework. She makes them give her money and lunch tickets. She makes the boys steal make-up from a department store. 7: Natalie says that the class is really afraid of the bully.
**2. a)** Jeremy: D, F, B, C, E, A
Natalie: C, B, E, D, F, A
**b)** Jeremy: A: alone; B: stop talking; C: rude words; D: same again; E: hands off year 7; F: gay
Natalie: A: gang; B: homework; C: birthday money; D: threats; E: hit; F: stealing

## 5 Dead boring

**1.** 1. Sheila doesn't like this lesson. She is bored, because they are doing a revision for their exams in November. 2. Pedro is not a Spanish, but a Mexican boy. 3. The story starts on a Monday morning, but she had met Pedro before Monday. 4. The narrator's name is Sheila Alington, not Sharon. 5. Sheila has to write down her teacher's words. 6. Sheila has to write the restrictions 30 times, once for each minute she has been dreaming. 7. Pedro's parents came to the U.S.A. 10 years ago,. That's a long time, not a short time ago. 8. Her great-grandparents came from Europe. 9. In the end she does not throw her lines away, she writes across all of them article 1 and 2 of the Universal Declaration of Human Rights.

**2. Lösungsvorschlag:**
Sheila Alington, blonde, blue-eyed, good-looking, is sitting in her classroom. Her books are in front of her. As it is October 2038, the classroom looks different. There are computers on tables everywhere, a big TV on the wall, so that you can see the person who you want to talk to (headmaster, caretaker, network administrator etc.)
Sheila and her classmates are sitting at group tables. Sheila's table is near the window so that she can look out of it and see the sun shining.
Flashback: Sheila meets Pedro, a typically Mexican-looking boy – dark-skinned, black-haired, brown-eyed, strong-looking – in the street, where she has dropped all her shopping.
During the flashback the teacher's voice is continuously heard in the background. The last words 'restrictions and Sheila Alington' are to be heard precisely and loudly.
Change of scene: back in class. Teacher, female, old, skinny, wrinkled, unfriendly, dressed in grey and black, glasses, standing in front of Sheila who is looking up at her, speaking sharply.
After Sheila's answer you can guess from the teacher's face what she is thinking: angry, hurt, offended. Her way of talking when she repeats the restrictions is very slow, very clear. She sounds a bit like a robot.
When the teacher announces what Sheila has got to do she is almost whispering, she talks in a very low voice which makes the class dead quiet. Nobody moves for about 5 seconds. Teacher leaves class.
Change of scene: Sheila at home, lying on her bed in her room talking to Pedro on the phone. In front of her sheets of paper on which you can see the quotation from the Universal Declaration in red. The copied lines are written in blue. Sheila tells Pedro what happened.
Change of scene:
Sheila hands in her lines to her teacher, who takes it and looks at it.
In class Sheila is called to the headmaster's over the TV on the wall. She is asked to bring her things.
Sheila at the headmaster's: her parents are present. She gets expelled (angry discussions, reproaches).

**3. Lösungsvorschlag:**
I don't like Pedro's comment, because he is wrong. Sooner or later Sheila would come into conflict with what is taught at her school. But it is typical of Pedro, still feeling like a foreigner to consider that what happened to Sheila as his fault. His self-esteem is not very strong. He thinks Sheila did it for him. But this is not true, she did it for herself, because she found out that the restrictions mean discrimination against all foreigners and that integration is the way to treat people who come to the USA.
I don't like the mother's comment. You can guess what she really wants to say: that Pedro is responsible for what has happened. She doesn't seem to like him, because she says that

# Lösungen und HV-Texte

Pedro is not the right person for her daughter. She wishes her daughter to be together with Americans. So she draws the line between immigrants and Americans.
The teacher's comment shows that she is very <u>superficial</u>. She has not taken the trouble to even ask Sheila why she <u>quoted</u> from the Declaration of Human Rights. I think she can't <u>be bothered with</u> what has happened.
I like the grandmother's statement. She is on Sheila's side and she <u>blames</u> the teacher who doesn't seem to care.
I can't understand Sheila's friend. Her comment shows that she has got a lot of prejudices. If my friend was in trouble I would support him/her. I think Sheila's friend hides herself behind her parents' restrictions. Maybe she is afraid of being <u>expelled</u>, too, if she says that what Sheila did is all right.

**4.** *Denkbar:*
- sometimes criminals <u>enter</u> the country illegally, they can be sent back
- immigrants take German people's jobs away
- adult children should not be allowed to <u>enter</u> the country <u>automatically</u>
- taxes could be spent on important things and not on social <u>welfare</u> for immigrants who don't want to work

*cons:*
- there are a lot of people in poor countries who can't <u>survive</u> where they live
- our lives would be poor without immigrants who open restaurants and special food shops
- it's important and interesting to find out about the culture and the religion of immigrants
- immigrants teach us not to <u>take</u> everything we've got <u>for granted</u>
- immigrants often do jobs no one else wants to do
- a rich country like Germany must support people who <u>flee</u> from war
- We need specialists from other countries (India) to help e.g. with Information Technology

## Topic 3

### 1 Addicted to the Internet

**1.** *Denkbar:*
The diary extracts deal with a girl named Karen who uses the Internet night after night. When her parents get a telephone bill for £90 they get very angry. They try to talk to her but they don't get through to her. Karen and her parents have a <u>row</u> and her father tells her she will have to sell her computer to repay the money. Karen packs her things, takes her diary and she steals £150 from her mother's purse. Karen goes to London and meets an Internet friend there. His girlfriend makes Karen send an e-mail to her parents to say she is all right. Karen's mother is very worried and doesn't know what to do.

**2. a)** Internet, to chat, to contact, disconnected, chat room, to switch off, telephone bill, e-mail, to turn off
**b)** *Denkbar:* screen, mouse, mouse pad, web, CD-ROM, search engine, file, music files, scanner, to scan, printer, to print, modem, drive, hard disc, memory, hardware, software, note-book
**c)** *Denkbar:* e-mail: An e-mail is sort of a digital/or electronic/letter. You can send it from one computer to another. Within a minute your partner can read it.
to chat: You can write or talk to people on the Internet
to contact: You try to find/meet someone on the Internet
telephone bill: While you are connected to the Internet, telephone costs <u>arise</u> and you have to pay the bill.

chat room: Here you can meet people <u>virtually</u> who want to talk about the same topic.

**3. Lösungsvorschlag:**
Someone who is addicted lives in his or her own world. He/she doesn't react to anything that keeps him/her off the dream world he or she is living in. So Karen doesn't realize that her parents want to talk to her about a serious problem. That's why Karen's mother writes that her husband 'didn't get through to her …' (Mum l. 12).
Another symptom for Karen's <u>addiction</u> is that "she has changed" (Mum ll. 17–18). And that her mum <u>states</u> that she seems to be "on drugs" (Mum l. 18). Her mother's description of Karen's change <u>proves</u> that Karen isn't herself any more. Even when she sees the amount of money her parents have to pay she <u>denies</u> this to be true ("It can't be that much" Karen ll. 23–24). She doesn't face facts even when she is <u>confronted</u> with them ("I don't really know if she realizes the amount of money her Internet-hobby costs" Mum ll. 23–25) and her mum sees that she lives in a world far away from her <u>former self</u> ("My friendly and optimistic daughter looks and behaves like a zombie" Mum ll. 20–21).
When Karen finds out that she hasn't got a computer any more because her parents took it away, she panics: she has got to find someone who will let her use the computer. ("I must find another one." Karen ll. 30–31) And that's why she doesn't ask a friend or her cousin Phil for help but runs away to an Internet friend who she hardly knows ("He wasn't happy to see me because he is living with his girlfriend" Karen ll. 34–35). When it turns out that Duncan does not live in the same <u>virtual</u> world as Karen, she realizes for the first time that she has got a big problem. But her problem is that Duncan won't allow her to use his computer. Because she's addicted she can only think of herself, not about her parents, who might worry, and not about how she can <u>survive</u> in London. She writes an e-mail to her parents because she is told to do so ("Nina made me write a e-mail to my parents" Karen ll. 39–40), not because it is her own wish to <u>calm</u> her parents <u>down</u>.
All in all you can say that there are a lot of symptoms that show that Karen is addicted. She might <u>recover</u> if Internet <u>access</u> is stopped for a while. Then she might be able to realize what has happened and what she has been doing.

**4.** 1. is sitting; 2. tries, loves; 3. is talking; 4. gets; 5. tells, is talking; 6. is not answering; 7. writes, is planning; 8. decides

### 2 A meeting with Phil

HV-Text: 47 – 48
*Karen has been surfing on the Internet day and night for months. When her parents get a £900 phone bill, Karen has a huge argument with them and runs away from home. Her 21-year-old cousin Phil, who showed her how to use the Internet, gets an e-mail from Karen. She wants to talk to him. They meet in a cafe – somewhere in London.*

*Phil:* Hi, Karen!
*Karen:* Hi, Phil! Sorry I'm late, but I had to make sure you were alone.
*Phil:* Why don't you trust me? I keep my promises. Forgotten that? Now, sit down and get that wild look out of your eyes. There's nothing to worry about.
What will you have?
*Karen:* Nothing. Thanks!
*Phil:* When did you last eat?
*Karen:* Dunno!
*Phil:* Here, have my sandwich. I haven't touched it yet.
*Karen:* (munching) Have you got any money with you?
*Phil:* Just a minute, Karen. Let's get one or two things straight first. You told me, you wanted to talk, so let's do that for a start.
*Karen:* What about?
*Phil:* I don't know, you asked me to come down to London, didn't you?

*Karen:* Would you have come if I had told you I wanted money?
*Phil:* No!
*Karen:* See?
*Phil:* No, but if I had known …
*Karen:* I need some money!
*Phil:* What for?
*Karen:* I'll pay it back. I don't want to steal from you or my parents.
*Phil:* Right! How are you going to pay it back? Selling drugs? Stealing from other people? Prostitution?
*Karen: (shouting and crying)* I can't stop, Phil, I just can't !
*Phil:* What do you mean you can't stop?
*Karen: (voice still shaking)* Look, I'm usually online about 16 hours a day, and it doesn't seem to be enough.
*Phil:* Listen, Karen, the first thing you should know is that there are flat rates. You pay a certain amount of money, it is less than £30 a month, and you can use the Internet as often as you want to. Why didn't you talk to me before running away ?
*Karen:* We had this terrible argument! I just had to get away from my parents.
*Phil:* Second thing: I know all about chat rooms. Did you know there are people whose job it is keep you in the chat room by answering every single thing? Believe me, I am one of them. I know how to keep customers and I am very successful. And the pay isn't bad.
*Karen:* So, the whole thing isn't real ?
*Phil:* Of course, not. It has nothing to do with real life. Making money, that's what it's all about.
*Karen:* I don't believe you, Phil.
*Phil:* Look, as soon as we get home, I'll show you. So let's get your things and go home
*Karen:* But what am I going to tell my parents?
*Phil:* Don't worry, They'll just be so pleased to have you back. Now come on … *(fade)*

1. 3, 5, 8, 10, 7, 2, 9, 1, 4, 6

**2. Lösungsvorschlag:**
Karen meets her cousin Phil in a cafe in London. She pretends that she wants to meet him because she wants to talk to him. But it turns out that she wants money which she offers to pay back. When Phil doubts that she will ever be able to pay the money back, Karen admits that she is addicted to the Internet. Phil informs his cousin about the virtual world of the Internet. At first Karen doesn't believe him, but then she agrees to go back to her parents with Phil, although she is worried about how to explain everything to them. But Phil calms her down and says that they will be happy to see her.

**3. Lösungsvorschlag:**
I think it is a good thing that Phil comes alone and does not confront Karen e.g. with her mum. Karen knows that she is in the wrong, but she cannot admit that she is worried. When he offers her his sandwich, Phil behaves like an adult would do – like her parents. He is strict, he doesn't offer her any money. He doesn't tell her that he would not help her – even with a certain amount of money – but he reminds her of the e-mail she wrote to him asking for a possibility to talk. By taking her seriously he treats her like an adult on the one hand, on the other hand he shows her that he cares about her.
When he points out that she would owe him money and would not able to pay it back she he gets her to the point where she breaks down. She tells him about her problem, about being obsessed with the Internet.
Phil doesn't condemn the Internet, but he tells her how she can manage without the enormous costs (flat rates).
When he explains to her that most of her Internet partners are fakes like himself he shows her the virtual world of the Internet and at the same time hints at the real world – her parents who love her and want her back. At the end of the dialogue he promises to prove what he has been telling her. Karen is curious enough to want to know and, moreover, she has been looking for a way to get back into the world of her childhood where she is safe. And Phil will help her to find her way back.

## 3 Work experience at British Airways

**2 a)** polite ending 9 – what Kevin expects the company to do 8 – the date 3 – signature 11 – why Kevin is writing 5 – name and address of the company Kevin is writing to 2 – what is sent with the letter 12 – how Kevin addresses the person he is writing to 4 – formal ending 10 – Kevin's address 1 – what qualifications Kevin has got for the job 6 – when Kevin wants to start and finish working and why he wants to get the job 7

**b)**

Kevin Wegemann
Schlosshofstr. 43
33615 Bielefeld
Germany
Tel.: 0521/64374

British Airways
POBox 123456
London W 12 3 PT
UK

20th February 2001

Dear Sir or Madam,
I am writing to apply for a period of work experience at your office in London.
I am at present in Year 11 of Martin-Niemöller-Gesamtschule in Bielefeld, and I am going to specialize in English and Information Technology in Year 12. After my A-levels I intend to study Information Technology. For work experience in Years 9 and 10 I worked at a computer shop and at a travel agent's.
I would like to use the period from July 2nd to August 31st of the summer holidays before Year 12 to improve my English and experience a little of the world of your work. Should you offer me the chance to work in your company I would be very grateful if you could help me to find accomodation.
I look forward to hearing from you soon.
Yours sincerely
Kevin Wegemann

Enclosed: CV, copy of last report

## 4 Is Tupac still alive?

**1. Lösungsvorschlag:**
1 East Flamingo Road; 2 Shakur's car; 3 Suge Knight was driving; 4 Tupac Shakur (passenger); 5 white Cadillac; 6 gunman; 7 Las Vegas Strip; 8 East Flamingo Road was busy; 9 Tupac's car was accompanied by about 10 cars, in some of them were his bodyguards.

**2. Lösungsvorschlag:**
1. Why didn't Tupac's bodyguards follow the gunmen in the white Cadillac?
– Some of the bodyguards actually tried to follow the white Cadillac, but the street was very busy and there were several white Cadillacs.
2. Why didn't the police make efforts to find the white Cadillac?
– By the time police realized there was a shooting, too much time had gone by.
3. Why didn't Suge Knight talk to the press?
– He was in shock and treated in hospital, because he was injured. Apart from that he maybe felt threatened as well. But there are rumours that Suge Knight organized the murder.
4. Why was Tupac without his bullet-proof vest?
– Bad luck. Maybe he just forgot to put it on.
5. Why did Tupac want to disappear from public view?
Every now and then stars want to disappear. They earn a lot of money, but they also have to give up their private life. Another reason might be that he felt threatened. Tupac had committed crimes, had been arrested eight times and had spent eight months in prison. He often said that he expected

he'd die before he reached 30.
6. Did Tupac fake his own death?
– Some people say he did, so that he could disappear from public view. In prison he read a lot of books by and about Macchiavelli who disappeared to trick his enemies.

**3. Lösungsvorschlag:**
– It's hard to believe that someone is dead at the age of 25. Tupac was very young.
– Tupac was only at the beginning of his career. Fans can't accept that he will not record music any more.
– After Tupac's death a lot of his records have been <u>released</u>, but that is not unusual, because music companies know that a <u>violent</u> death is good for business.
– Tupac was <u>idolized</u> by his fans, and a god cannot die.
– As his music is still alive <u>among</u> his fans – you can hear Tupac singing and there are videos – you get the illusion that he himself must be alive somewhere.

**4.** *Denkbar:*
– I could try the Internet. With the help of search engines (e.g. Altavista, Google) I could get a lot of information.
– If I wanted to get the lyrics of some of his songs, I'd have to go to music sites and look for them.
– If I wanted to talk about Tupac or if I had questions, I could try people in chat rooms.
– I could buy Cathy Scott's book 'The Killing of Tupac Shakur' and read it.
– I could listen to his music on CDs or on MP3 downloads.
– I could look at CD covers and get information from them.
– I could try a modern music dictionary.

## 5 The key to the future

**1. a)** They are sitting at a table, the gypsy is telling the businessman about his future. There is a glass ball and some playing cards on the table. The gypsy is holding a playing card (<u>Ace</u> of Hearts) in one hand and a mobile phone (key) to her ear.
**b)** A mobile phone in the <u>shape</u> of a key
**c)** The glass ball is the gypsy's <u>tool</u>. In it she pretends to see the customer's future.
The playing cards are special ones. Some people believe if the customer mixes them and the fortune teller <u>deals</u> them, she can tell their meaning to the customer and <u>predict</u> the customer's future.

**2.** *Denkbar:*
The company which is called Calyafone offers mobile phones with special services like telling you your horoscope of the day. They give you headlines, news or weather reports. They inform you about sports and the lottery results as well. All this is free for a year. This mobile phone can be your personal reminder, too. And you can also make use of these services on your ordinary telephone. If you want to become a customer, you can either send an e-mail or phone a certain number.

**3. Lösungsvorschlag:**
I think it was chosen because of the <u>familiar</u> sound. You simply MUST buy 'key' because it is something as necessary as food. You can't do without it, if you want to be happy and successful. <u>Moreover</u>, to say 'key is ready' means that it has just been created, that it is new and that the customer must buy it, because he/she wants to be in and must be up-to-date.

**4. Lösungsvorschlag:**
I think it was a very good idea to choose the picture of the <u>fortune-teller</u>, because she talks to you about the future. And in the future you will need this special service to be as well-informed as your partners at work. Of course, everybody knows that playing cards and glass balls are <u>fake</u> as far as telling the future is <u>concerned</u>, but the advertisement wants customers to <u>associate</u> their mobile phone with a thing everybody will have in the future. So, to be successful you need this service. The second message that is given with the <u>fortune-teller</u> is <u>happiness</u>. She offers herself as the 'Queen of Hearts.' Of course, the businessman in the picture knows she is not the one he has been looking for, but the company wants their customers to believe that if they have this service, it will be easy to keep good relationships with the people they like or love. The advertisement turns to two things people want to <u>achieve</u>: to lead a successful business life and to have a happy relationship with someone they love.
Although customers will easily understand that something is promised (success and happiness) which the company cannot keep, they will get the message: this mobile phone service is necessary if you want to be successful and happy. The company sells the key to you, but you have to make use of it, you have to <u>unlock</u> the door yourself.

**5. a)** *Linda:* Doctors, firemen and policemen always used walkie-talkies.
*John:* Yes, but they often didn't reach very far…
*Sue:* Then, in the beginning of the 90s businessmen sometimes used mobile phones. And in the mid 90s especially young men carried them around, even if they never used them.
*Kirsty:* I've always got it with me and I never go out without it.
*Pete:* I sometimes switch it off.

**b) Lösungsvorschlag:**
I couldn't do without my mobile phone. I can hardly remember a time without it. My father told me a story about when I was about 3 years old and swallowed a Lego brick. He had to call the doctor but our phone at home didn't <u>work</u> so he had to try to find a telephone box which was not damaged. I think a mobile phone is such a useful thing, if you can't get through to the person you want to talk to, you can simply leave a message over SMS. I think it is necessary to have a mobile phone on you, because if there is an accident or your car breaks down you can inform people quickly. My parents don't want me to leave the house without my mobile, because I've got to tell them if I'm home later than planned or if I can't be in for a meal. So they don't have to worry any more.
All in all you can say that mobile phones make life much easier and more comfortable.

## Topic 4

### 1 I believe in You!

**1.** *Years 1–4:* Martin is a brilliant student
*Year 5:* His mother dies of cancer, his father not interested
*Years 6–7:* Martin is a bully and very bad at school
*Year 8:* He joins Mrs White's class
*Year 9:* Martin's school work is getting much better, although he is not a good student
*end of Year 10:* Martin gets some GCSEs
*3 years apprenticeship:* Martin starts and finishes his apprenticeship as a dental technician
*5–6 years at university:* Martin studies at university and becomes a dentist
*after university:* Martin marries and gets his doctor's degree. His wife is going to have a baby girl.

**2. Lösungsvorschlag:**
When Martin is 11 years old he asks Mrs White if he can be in her class. She does not like the boy because he is a bully and she is worried because she thinks he will be a trouble maker. But because she is too busy, she agrees to take him into her class. The truth is that she is <u>moved</u> by Martin's explanation of his <u>wish</u>. A reason for her interest can be seen in the fact that she wants to find out more about him, and she learns Martin lives without love. Martin's birthday present, the bunch of wild flowers, shows that Martin wants his teacher to be a <u>substitute</u> for his mum. Mrs White understands his

# Lösungen und HV-Texte

explanation and accepts that she is a sort of second mum for Martin. That's why she makes sure that there are always wild flowers in her classroom. By doing so she gives Martin the feeling of being at home in the classroom, at school and with her.

The next key situation is when Mrs White tells Martin that she is worried about going to the dentist. Maybe this is true, but why should a teacher tell an 11 or 12-year-old student about her weakness? By doing so she asks him for help. And helping is the opposite of bullying. By admitting that she needs him as much as he needs her, she achieves two things: on the one hand Martin's father gets a different impression of his son (he is no longer the bully teachers used to complain about), on the other hand Mrs White accepts Martin as a partner, as a son who can help her. They share a secret, Mrs White's weakness. That is the point when Martin starts to learn again and makes up for a lot of lost time.

At the end of the story he says thank you to her, a thing he could not have done before, and by naming his baby daughter after her, he admits that she has helped him to stay out of trouble ("Thank you for believing in me.").

Mrs White's last sentences refer to the situation when Martin was 12 years old, holding her hand at the dentist's. She does what she has always done: she makes Martin feel important. Maybe she still feels a bit ashamed that she didn't want Martin to join her class at first. She pretends that she is selfish, but by becoming Martin's patient she continues what she started a long time ago: she supports him.

### 3. Lösungsvorschlag:

When my cousin was about 15 years old, he really got into trouble with his Maths teacher. My cousin is Curdish like me, and the trouble is, once we get angry we can't control ourselves well. I don't like it and I try to keep cool all the time, but sometimes I get so angry that I can understand Nezir, my cousin. This is what happened: During a Maths lesson his teacher had been picking on him. He had forgotten his homework, he was late for the lesson. She she was dead right. But did she ask for a reason? No, she didn't. Nezir couldn't concentrate on the tasks they were doing because there had been a fight. And after the third time she asked him a question he couldn't answer, he got really furious. It had nothing to do with her, but he jumped up, the table fell over, so did his chair and he was about to leave the class, when she stopped him. He clenched his fists to control himself. That's when she said she got scared. Parents' and teachers' meeting. They were about to expel him from school, when I thought of my class teacher. She talked to Nezir and she promised to defend him. By doing so she got into trouble with her fellow teachers, but she didn't mind. In the end Nezir was able to stay at our school, and she achieved what nobody else did: he is on time for his lessons now, he has got all his homework and his books, and he does not cut classes any more. And believe it or not, in a few months he will get some GCSEs and start an apprenticeship. I don't know how she managed it, but my cousin has changed.

**4.** 1. will be sitting, 2. will be looking, 3. will be talking, 4. will have forgotten, 5. will have invited, 6. will have spoken, 7. will have told

## 2 The key to a happy marriage

**1.** *name:* Jerry Collins
*profession:* professor of marriage and family studies
*important statements about marriage:* love simply isn't enough; you shouldn't marry the person you love if the results of the questionnaire differ radically
*name:* Betty French
*profession:* marriage guidance counsellor
*important statements about marriage:* you can never predict the success of a marriage; life will teach you if you can go on living together, not a questionnaire
*name:* Deirdre Dawkins
*profession:* family lawyer
*important statements about marriage:* the divorce rate is high because people mary for all sorts of reasons; the questionnaire will not put her out of business

### 2. Lösungsvorschlag:

Love is the most important thing in my life.
Money is important, too.
Married couples can have different hobbies.
I don't want to have babies during the first four years of our marriage.
We should talk before buying something for the house.
We should each have a lot of different friends, even if we don't like each other's friends.
Mothers should stay at home with their babies because they have a more natural relationship with them.
It must be possible to talk to my friends about the problems I have with my wife/my husband.
Relationships change, we change, so to break up if our marriage doesn't work is something natural.
It is important to agree on our children's education.
We must like each other's parents and relatives.
If there are children we should stay together, even if our marriage doesn't work any more, because children suffer from divorce.
I would not mind if my partner had a girl or boyfriend as long as it doesn't affect my marriage.

### 3. Lösungsvorschläge:

*pros:*
– it could help me to find out if I agree or disagree on basic thoughts like having children, money, hobbies, friends;
– it could help me to find out about myself – maybe I've never thought about the things I'm asked;
– it may be useful to talk to my partner about the things I was asked in the questionnaire;
– it might help me to find a more realistic view of my partnership

*cons:*
– if a couple is determined to get married they won't split up because of their differing answers to the questionnaire;
– you can't predict all the difficulties in life you have to cope with;
– if a couple wants to get married and gets a negative result from the questionnaire, their relationship might be affected;
– if people are really in love, a partner could consider the questionnaire a lack of confidence

*Alternative 1:*
I don't think I would do such a questionnaire for different reasons. First of all I disagree with Professor Collins because I think love can make up for a lot of faults you find with your partner. And I am aware of the fact that my partner will find faults with me, too. I know that I often react emotionally without thinking too much, on the other hand I know that my partner takes too long to make a decision. So we've got to find a way. I think it is ridiculous to do such a questionnaire because my boyfriend and me wouldn't split up just because we found out that we disagree on some things. I think Betty French is right: Life will teach you if you can cope with all the situations you get into. I'm of the opinion it's even dangerous to do such a questionnaire because if it turns out that my partner and I have got completely different results, it can be a sort of self-fulfilling prophecy if our marriage doesn't work.
If my partner asked me to do such a questionnaire, I would consider it a lack of confidence. I'd have the feeling he didn't trust me any more and that would be the end of our love.
All in all I think the questionnaire does more damage than good.

*Alternative 2:*
I think I would agree to do a questionnaire to find out about myself and my partner.
My parents are divorced and a lot of their friends are, too. It was hard on me when my parents told me that my dad would not live with us any more. At the age of 8 you don't understand why a couple splits up and you consider it to be your own fault, although they keep telling you that it isn't. If

my parents had done a questionnaire before getting married, they would have found out that they didn't agree on most of the things mentioned in the questionnaire. My father is a withdrawn scientist who is interested in nature, my mother is only happy when there are friends or relatives around who she can talk to. Maybe that's why I'm very careful in choosing a partner or making friends. There's always that broken marriage I have in mind and I think it would be terribly unfair on any children if there is a chance that we could break up. And this is something I could find out with the questionnaire. When I read the article, I realized that this was a problem for me. Now I can talk to my partner or friends about it and later I can find out if my partner can accept that I am so careful. Maybe there are reasons why my partner reacts in a way I can't understand either and this could serve as a basis for a good understanding and relationship.

**4.** loves doing – tut gern; sends … love – lässt … grüßen; We'd love to visit you – wir würden uns freuen, euch zu besuchen; for love nor money – nicht für Geld und gute Worte; love of helping – Freude am Helfen; for love – umsonst; the love of her life – die große Liebe ihres Lebens; no love lost – sie können sich nicht ausstehen; love bite – Knutschfleck; love – seine Liebste; With our love – mit herzlichen Grüßen/Alles Liebe

## 3 Fly me into Space

**1.** *Denkbar:*
1. Part of the training was an emergency simulation. Susan had the check list and told the others which buttons to press.
2. Susan and one of the boys, Tad, liked each other a lot from the start.
3. There was an exercise in a huge tank to train using oxygen bottles. Susan had problems with her bottle. Tad signalled to the other boys to bring Susan up to the surface.
4. Susan got to the surface. She was all right and Tad held her in his arms. A coach from Nasa found out that a pipe on Susan's air bottle was damaged.
5. During take-off training they sat in a seat which was shot up to a platform. Two of the boys were frightened but Susan wasn't because she knew that Tad was waiting for her at the top.
6. At the farewell-party for their work experience in the cafeteria, Tad took Susan's passport out of her pocket while he was kissing and dancing with her. He didn't want her to go home.
7. The following day when Susan wanted to check in at the airport, she realized that she had not got her passport. The passport officer was angry, but Tad and the other boys were there to say goodbye and Tad gave Susan her passport back.
8. Back home in Britain Susan got an e-mail from Tad and sent one back to him. They missed each other a lot.

**2. a)** *Denkbar:*
1. Try again, Tad, press the green button, please! 2. Sorry, Tad, you told us you would check the equipment, but I should have double-checked it. 3. Look, it doesn't look that bad, and Tad has survived. Do you want me to go next? 4. Would you mind being a bit more careful with me? I'll die from lack of oxygen in a second, Tad. 5. I'm sorry, but I can't find my passport at the moment. I know the other passengers are waiting, but I'm sure I'll find it in a minute.

**b)** *Lösungsvorschlag:*
1. Sorry, Susan, I got it all wrong. Can you forgive me? 2. I'm so sorry, Susan. I just didn't see that pipe for the oxygen was damaged. It's all my fault. 3. Yes, please, if you don't mind. 4. Sorry, but I'm so pleased you're alive! 5. Don't worry and take your time. The plane won't go without you and your passport!

**3.** *Lösungsvorschlag:*
An astronaut can get into such difficult situations that he/she is simply dependent on the other group members. Let's take Susan's group. They started off with the simulation of an emergency in the rocket. In a situation like that there is not much time to discuss everything. Nearly always someone takes the lead and gives orders which the others carry out without asking why. You must be able to rely on the other team or group members.
The leaders of a group will change according to the difficulties the group is in because each one of the astronauts is an expert. When Susan could not be the leader, Tad organized her rescue. Or when Tad stole Susan's passport, the other two boys made him give it back to her.
I think it is important that astronauts are trained to trust in each other's skills and capabilities. You shouldn't try to find the best solution yourself. You must be able to admit that your partner's solution is the better one for the team.
Team spirit is something that must be developed, too. A team is a sort of family, they'll tell you what is wrong or right and they'll help you to get a sense of belonging.
16 teenagers did the work experience, but you only get to know something about Susan and the three boys because they are a team.
I can imagine that a team of astronauts is trained the same way as Susan and the three boys were and I think that sometimes a very good expert may not be taken by Nasa because of his lack of team spirit.

**4.** *Lösungsvorschläge:*
*Alternative 1:*
I would like to do work experience at the U.S. Space and Rocket Center. First of all I think it must be great to meet people with the same interests, and I am interested in space. Wow! When I was a little girl I always wanted toys that had to do with space, such as Lego rockets and all the films about Star Trek. I did not know about the possibility of doing work experience in the States, otherwise I would have tried myself. Maybe I can do that after I have finished school. I am sure my parents would help me to pay for it and I've saved some money, too. I would like to spend my time with people who have the same interests, because my friends all laugh at me: a girl who is interested in space. It's true, it was different when I was little, because I had lots of boyfriends who liked space as well. But they seem to have grown out of it. So I tried the Internet and I found some friends there, but they are all male, and they turn funny if they find out that I am of the opposite sex. So what's wrong with being interested in rockets and spaceships, I'd like to know? I think the things Susan experienced are simply fascinating – to be trained as an astronaut. There are women who are astronauts, aren't there?

*Alternative 2:*
My answer to that question is simply "no". And there are several reasons: first of all there are the costs. Susan's parents must be very well off, because the flight to the U.S. Space and Rocket Center must cost an enormous amount of money. Moreover I'd have to pay for my stay and I'd need pocket money as well.
Another reason is that I'm not interested in spaceships and rockets at all. To learn about the technical details of these things is boring and I'm neither interested in Physics nor in Computer Technology. Sure, it seems exciting to be trained in how to survive in a dangerous situation like Susan was in the tank. But I think I can do that elsewhere – e.g. on a good diving course.
The last reason is that I would not like to be all on my own. During our work experience my classmates and I used to meet during breaks or after work. And there was a lot we had to tell each other. I would not like to miss that. Sure, I could talk to the other people at the Space and Rocket Center, but it would be in English all the time, a subject I am not very good at. And the people would only be team mates, no one I'd really know well. I think it's terrible if you fall in love and there isn't a good friend around to talk to – not even my parents or brothers and sisters.
All in all I'd say I would not like to do work experience like that.

## 4 Three girls out

1. ... Tim and his sister Val ... are on holiday.
2. ... are too young for the party.
3. ... they don't know that they are getting alcoholic drinks.
4. ... is a drug-dealer.
5. ... smoke a joint.
6. ... the police knock on the door/Jake asks Tim to get his sister Val.
7. ... find a lot of drugs/speed, ecstasy, hash and cocaine.
8. ... Carlene to go to the toilet.
9. ... are taken to the police station.
10. ... she can go to the toilet at the police station.

**2. Lösungsvorschlag:**
1. It was because they probably knew that their parents would not give them permission.
2. It was because he wanted to find some new customers for his drugs.
3. Kevin probably wants to get the girls drunk as soon as possible.
4. It's because after what Kevin and Val said, they have to prove that they are old enough for that party.
5. Either he wants to show off, or he intends to have an affair with her. Perhaps she wants her to smoke his joint without thinking about what she is smoking.
6. They must have information that there are drugs at the party; maybe they know that Tim is a drug-dealer.
7. It's because Tim told his friends not to say anything. The police could have asked the party guests their names and addresses at Tim's house.
8. Maybe she thinks Carlene would try to run away. Perhaps she thinks Carlene wants to throw drugs down the toilet.

**3. Lösungsvorschlag:**
I am not sure how I would have reacted. I think it is a big thing for girls of their age to be invited to a party by someone so much older than they are. Curiosity might be one reason and a sense of adventure. It makes you feel uncomfortable on the one hand, but it is the thrill that might keep you there. You realize quite well that you should leave, but as you are easily bored at that age, you might have the feeling that you'll miss something you could tell your friends about later and show off about it. I think the girls have got mixed feelings right from the beginning, otherwise they would have told their parents about the party.

**4. Lösungsvorschlag:**
*Policewoman:* Did you find the toilet, love?
*Carlene:* Yes, thank you. What – what are you going to do now?
*Policewoman:* Don't worry. We'll phone your mum in a minute. She'll fetch you and then you can go home.
*Carlene:* Can't you get my dad? It would make things much easier!
*Policewoman:* Anyway, the sooner we start, the sooner we can call your parents, okay? So what's your name?
*Carlene:* Carlene Jones.
*Policewoman:* You are shaking all over. Can I get you a cup of tea?
*Carlene:* No, thank you, but a glass of water would be fine.
*Policewoman:* Here you are. Now, what's your address, please?
*Carlene:* It's 59, Wingfield Road, Bishop Auckland PT3 OP6. Our telephone number is 01388 for Bishop Auckland 47003.
*Policewoman:* Got it. Now tell me, how long have you known Tim Wilkes?
*Carlene:* He was changing light bulbs at our school when he spoke to us. We talked for a while and he told us he was giving a party on Sunday and wouldn't we like to come. He gave us his address and phone number.
*Policewoman:* Now tell me, how come you smoked dope?
*Carlene:* Someone offered it. I can't even remember who.
*Policewoman:* All right then. Let's call your parents. If you remember anything, please come back and let us now. Okay? You can wait over there. Bye
*Carlene:* Bye.

## 5 After the party

HV-Text: 49 – 52
*Clare, Sue and Carlene went to a party without telling their parents. There was alcohol and everyone was smoking joints at the party. At two o'clock in the morning the police search the house and take all the young people to the police station. The three girls' mums collect the girls after they have been questioned by the police.*

1.
*Clare:* Mum, I didn't mean to ...
*Mum:* Shhh. Let's get to bed. We can talk about it tomorrow.
*Clare:* But Mum, I must explain everything. I didn't know there were going to be drugs there, I'd never had a joint before.
*Mum:* Clare, it's not the drugs and the alcohol that I'm worried about; it's that you didn't tell me where you were going that hurts.
*Clare:* But I was sure you wouldn't let me go.
*Mum:* And would I have been wrong?
*Clare:* No, but there are things I have to find out for myself. That's what you keep telling me.
*Mum:* Right, but I didn't think that meant I'd have to pick you up at the police station.
*Clare:* I'm sorry about that, Mum. I didn't mean to upset you.
*Mum:* I know. That's why we can talk about it like adults, isn't it? I know my daughter so I'm not going to make you stay in for a month or anything like that. You'll have to face your friends at school on Monday and that's worse than anything I could do to you!
*Clare:* (sobbing) Mum, I really didn't mean to hurt you. I am sorry, I really am.

2.
*Mum:* There's only one thing I want to know, Sue. Why didn't you tell me about that party?
*Sue:* I wanted to, but it never seemed to be the right time. Do you know what I mean?
*Mum:* I know exactly what you mean, young woman. You knew very well that I'd say no. We don't even know the people who gave the party.
*Sue:* But I had been invited by this boy at school who I fancy ...
*Mum:* Fun, that's the only thing you wanted to have. Did you think about me, working all day, and now all this trouble. What do you think your teachers will say when they find out.
*Sue:* If nobody tells them ...
*Mum:* Oh, they'll be told, believe me.
*Sue:* Mum, Mum, the police won't tell anybody. I mean, I didn't have any drugs on me myself.
*Mum:* You didn't. But those people gave you a joint and you smoked it. Next thing they will ask you to deal in drugs for them. It always starts like that, doesn't it?
*Sue:* Sorry, Mum, but can I go to bed now? I know you are furious but I feel sick again.
*Mum:* Okay, then, go to bed, but remember there are people who have to work.

3.
*Carlene:* Mum?
*Mum:* I don't want to hear anything, Carlene. I just don't. I've got a terrible headache.
*Carlene:* But Mum, I'd like to explain ...
*Mum:* Something wrong with your ears or what? I don't want to hear anything. Best thing we can do is forget the whole thing.
*Carlene:* How can I forget? It was terrible. Just listen what happened to me ...
*Mum:* I told you, I don't want to hear anything. If you've got to ruin your life, just do it. But solve your problems, because I've got enough problems myself, believe me.
*Carlene:* Mum, I'd like to talk.
*Mum:* Okay. Dr. Appleton is a very nice doctor. Talk to him. And there are social workers and lots of teachers you can talk to at school. It's expensive enough, that private school, isn't it? Look, it's 3 o'clock in the morning. I've got an important meeting tomorrow morning, and then a

45

# Lösungen und HV-Texte

tennis match at 6 o'clock. What about sleeping on it?
*Carlene:* But Mum ...
*Mum:* Just to make it absolutely clear, I am too busy and too tired to do any talking. When I was young we talked to friends about all those little problems we had. Be a good girl and leave me alone, will you?
*Carlene:* Okay, Mum! See you tomorrow.

**1.** *Clare's mum:* – is hurt because her daughter didn't tell her about the party. (r); – wants to treat her daughter as an adult. (r); – wants to punish Clare. (w)
*Sue's mum:* – says that she knew Tim's parents. (w); – will tell Sue's teachers about the party. (r); – is angry because Sue only seems to think of herself. (r)

*Carlene's mum:* – is not really interested in her daughter's problems. (r); – tells Carlene that she has got a terrible stomach ache. (w); – asks Carlene to talk to somebody else. (r)

**2. Lösungsvorschlag:**
I don't like Carlene's mum at all. She is selfish and too much concerned about her own problems. She pretends to have a headache so she need not talk to her daughter. She doesn't realize that her daughter is in trouble and simply wants to talk about her problems. Carlene's mum pays for a good education, so she thinks she need not care about her daughter any more. She seems to lead a busy life in which there is no room for a child.
Sue's mum does not react much better. She is concerned about her own feelings. She is furious and angry with her daughter. But I can understand that reaction. Parents are angry with you, because they worry a lot about you. But that does not mean that they don't love you. You can see that Sue's mum is deeply worried because she imagines her daughter selling drugs. They always imagine the worst.
I really like Clare's mum. She tells her daughter that what she did was wrong, and she points out why she is hurt: her daughter didn't tell her the truth. So the lack of confidence is what really worries her, neither the alcohol nor the drugs. In the end Clare realizes what was wrong and tells her mum that she didn't want to hurt her feelings. She sees that she made a mistake, but it will not affect the relationship between mother and daughter.

**3. Denkbar:**
In the end of their dialogue Carlene is speechless, because her mother doesn't want to listen to her.
Carlene's mum is heartless, because she is not interested in her daughter's problems.
And Clare's mum is helpful, because she makes her daughter realize why she is hurt.
Sue feels helpless, because her explanation does not help her mother to get over her anger.
I think Tim is hateful because he only invited the girls to get them into the drug business.
Clare's mum is wonderful, because she treats her daughter like an adult.
Sue's mum thinks her daughter is not reliable.
Tim and his friends maybe think that taking drugs is fashionable.

# Topic 5

## 1 Just south of the border

**1.** 1. Juan was poor and hungry. He would have sold his watch to pay the doctor for his mum or help his little brothers and sisters who died. 2. Juan was not begging. 3. Juan was at the edge of the market. 4. Juan's brother was dirty and in rags. 5. The stall owner gave him some carrots and potatoes. 6. The stall with the meat was dirty with millions of flies. 7. Juan doesn't have a basket. 8. The butcher gave him a bone with bits of meat on it. 9. Juan smiled and whistled for his little brother.

**2.** *Juan:*
– about 15 years old
– is in rags
– face is dirty
– empty expression of hunger and hopelessness
– is very poor
– is happy if the stall owners give him food nobody wants
– doesn't speak English
– wants to find his father in the U.S.A.
*father:*
– left the family three years ago
– went to the U.S.A. illegally
– sent money home for three months
– his family hasn't heard from him since then
*mother:*
– used to work
– is ill now
– can't pay the doctor or buy medicine
– couldn't pay when three of her children were ill, so they died
*brothers and sisters:*
– his little brother is dirty
– is wearing rags
– is happy when he gets something to eat
– three of Juan's brothers and sisters died within three years

**3. Lösungsvorschlag:**
The boy is in tears, so he is sad. The reason could be that his older brother is no longer there. You get the impression that the relationship between the two brothers was very good (ll. 26–28). The little brother relied on his brother's skill to get little presents from the stall owners. He isn't sure if they will react the same way when they see he is alone. Another reason could be that now his brother has gone the feeding of his family is entirely up to him, and it seems too big a burden to carry. Up to now he was a child (the little boy skipping and happy, l. 27), but from now on he must be an adult, the eldest boy in the family. He has got responsibility. Maybe the loss of his older brother reminds him that he has lost his other brothers and sisters (Three of Juan's brothers and sisters had died during that time, ll. 44–45).
Seeing the little boy cry the narrator of the story feels guilty. I think he/she suddenly realizes what has happened. By giving Juan the money he or she has evoked dreams and illusions which probably will never come true for Juan! The narrator realizes that the money which she/he gave to Juan has caused unhappines in a family which so far has managed to survive. And there is not much she/he can do about it. That's why he/she feels guilty.

**4. Lösungsvorschlag:**
Juans runs away because for the first time in his life he has got a lot of money. He realizes the difference between himself and his family on the one hand and the foreigner who gives him money on the other hand. This foreigner can pay 10 dollars just to hear him say a few sentences. So he/she must come from a rich country, from the U.S.A., because he/she pays him in American money. And so that's his illusion: if a foreigner spends the amount of money that could help his family to survive a month for a few sentences, then it will be easy to earn enough money in that country to help his family. But Juan can't be sure he'll find a job and earn money. Maybe he

will be caught as an illegal immigrant and sent back to Mexico.
Juan probably dreams of finding his father, but this again is an illusion, because the U.S.A., is such a big country and he can't be sure at all that his father still lives at the place he last sent the money from. It is more realistic to suppose that his father found another woman.
But maybe Juan's dream of finding work will come true and he will be able to support his family.

**5. Lösungsvorschlag:**
I think in our country there are very poor families, too. And there are a lot of families without a father. But these families can live on social welfare. You don't get rich by living on it, but at least Juan and his brother would not have to beg for food or run around in dirty or torn clothes. I've got some classmates whose families don't earn money and who are supported by the state. They get money to live in decent flats and you cannot tell the difference between rich and poor by the way they dress. And of course, there is enough water, they can wash properly – nobody has to be dirty because of lack of water.
If a member of a poor family is ill, a doctor will treat him or her and they get the necessary medicine for free. So nobody has to die like Juan's little brothers and sisters because there was no medical help.
If Juan's mother was ill in our country there would be a home help who would look after her and her children. She would make sure the kids go to school and she would prepare the meals and even help the kids with their homework.
At the age of 15 Juan would still go to school and he would try to get a good apprenticeship. There would be no need for him to run away.

**6. a)** pay – payment; move – movement; happy – happiness; ill – illness; different – difference; ignore – ignorance; authentic – authenticity; illegal – illegality; beg – beggar; realize – realization
**b)** 1. authenticity, 2. beggar, 3. movements, 4. happiness 5. payment 6. ignorance, 7. difference, 8. illegality, 9. illness, 10. realization

## 2 Above the clouds

**1. a)** *Denkbar:*
*Virgin Atlantic offers ...*
– meet people and make new friends
– stopovers of up to five days
– see the world
– good pay
– free flights
– a pension (after a certain time)
– private medical insurance (after a certain time)
– long-term career chances
*Virgin Atlantic expects ...*
– energy
– initiative
– personality
– enthusiasm
– act as entertainer, safety officer and diplomat
– work for up to 13 hours (per flight)
– age: 19–30 years old
– taller than 5'2"
– good education
– EU passport
**b) Lösungsvorschläge:**
1. I understand that stopovers of five days are a maximum. Do you expect cabin crew to fly back non-stop after a 13-hour flight?
2. You said you pay good money. How much does a cabin crew member earn at the start?
3. How long does the certain time last, after which cabin crew get pension and private medical insurance?
4. What exactly do you understand by 'long-term career chances?
5. How many free flights a year do I get and where can I fly to?
6. What do you mean by a 'good education'? How many GCSEs do you expect or do I need any A-levels?

**2. Lösungsvorschläge:**
*Alternative 1:*
I'd like to do the job, because I think it's very exciting to visit all the places in the world which I've seen on TV or read about. I think it must be great to meet interesting or famous people on planes. It must be fun to help passengers with their meals, offer them drinks and talk to them. I like the way the cabin crew is dressed, but I think it must be hard to look fresh all the time on a 13-hour flight. But there is always make-up to help and I've seen cabin crew change their uniforms. And the pilots are always very good-looking in their uniforms, too, maybe one day a pilot will fall in love with me.
But what I like most about the job is that you can get free flights. So you can fly to the place you've already seen at work for free.
I don't mind working long hours, as long as I will be free afterwards. And that's what Virgin Atlantic offers: long working hours on the one hand, and up to 5 days off after that.
*Alternative 2:*
I would not like to work as a flight attendant for Virgin Atlantic, because I think it is as boring as working as a waiter or a waitress. What else do you do? You inform passengers about safety rules and you serve meals. Your time during a flight is so tight there is no time for long conversations with passengers, and the interesting or famous passengers will ignore you. Maybe it would be interesting to see exciting places, but I think after a while you will know everything, there won't be anything new. Moreover I think after a 13-hour flight you will be so tired that the only thing you will want to do is sleep. And I would hate to be dressed in a uniform all the time. I would not like to stay in hotels, I would miss my computer and most of all my friends and my family who I could hardly see.
All in all I can say that I would not enjoy to be a member of the cabin crew, but I would fancy a job on the ground. I could start in the mornings and finish at about 5.00 or 7.00 p.m. So there would be time enough to enjoy my free time.

**3. a) Lösungsvorschlag:**
– offer her a newspaper or a magazine
– offer her something to eat or drink
– ask her about the place she is going to
– or the place she is coming from
– offer her headphones for the film and tell her about what she is going to see
– ask her if she has enjoyed/is enjoying the meals
– ask her why she is travelling
– ask her if you bring her something to feel more comfortable
– ask her if she would like to listen to music
– ask her if she is enjoying the flight
– offer her help if she needs to go to the toilet
– show her how the reading light works
– ask her about the book she is just reading
**b) Lösungsvorschlag:**
*Flight attendant:* May I ask you what book you are reading?
*Lady:* Oh, it's only a children's book. It's Harry Potter.
*Flight attendant:* They're very good, aren't they. Let me show you how the reading lamp works. There you are. Is that better?
*Lady:* Yes, thank you very much. Have you read the book?
*Flight attendant:* No, I haven't, I'm afraid. But my little sister has read all the Harry Potter books. Do you like it?
*Lady:* Yes, it's fascinating. You know, I'm going to give it to my grandson as a birthday present.
*Flight attendant:* That's a good idea. You'll be able to talk about it with him later. How old is your grandson?
*Lady:* He's eleven, just the right age for Harry Potter!
**c)** 2. and 3. are the best endings because the flight attendant says she will come back again.

# Lösungen und HV-Texte

## 3 Why didn't I get the job?

HV-Text: 53 – 56
*A famous airline is looking for cabin crew. These three young people went for interviews but for some reason they weren't taken.*

*Lisa:*
I was so looking forward to that job, and I had prepared myself really well. I just don't know why they didn't take me. My name is Lisa, Lisa Hopkins and I will be 18 next May. I am not married. My mother is French and I speak English and French fluently; my German isn't bad either. If you look at my GCSEs, you'll see that I've got really good marks in languages. Okay, I'm not good at science, but I don't need Physics and Technology, do I? Was it so important that I couldn't explain the difference between newspapers like The Times and The Sun? I am just not interested in politics, sports and culture, and I told them I wasn't. The only thing I've ever seen cabin crew doing with newspapers is handing them out to passengers. Then they asked me if I always wear my safety belt when I'm driving a car. That hasn't anything to do with my application, has it?

*Helen:*
I'm Helen Baxter, I'm 21 and single. Well, I didn't get the job, but why, I'd like to know. The interviewer asked me all sorts of silly questions like: There has been a car accident. Injured people are still in the car. Suddenly the car starts to burn. What would you do? "You mustn't move injured persons," I told them. "I'd just hope the ambulance got there quickly." Then they asked: What would you do if you saw two teenagers fighting with knives? Call the police, of course. What else? What a silly question! Anyway people on planes don't have knives. The security people find things like that at the airport, don't they? Another question was: Imagine you are very tired but there is still very important work to do. How would you react? I told them that I'd go home and have a good night's sleep to be fresh for the remaining work the following morning. If I work when I'm tired, I get sick. What's wrong with sensible answers like that?

56 *Neil:*
I didn't apply for a job as a babysitter, did I? The only thing I wanted was to be part of the cabin crew. Me? Oh, I'm Neil Jenkins, and I am 28 years old. I'm an open and honest person. So was it wrong to tell the interviewer I didn't want to do the job all my life? Only two years or maybe three, to earn enough money to finish my studies at university. It would be hard to stay away from my wife and my baby son. But I really loved the idea of seven free flights a year. You see, my wife is Mexican, and every now and then she wants to see her family in Mexico. And flights are ever so expensive. I told them about my studies: I'm studying law and languages: French, Spanish, and Russian so I can get into international business later on. But I wanted to tell you the babysitter-situation. Imagine, they told me, imagine this situation: On a flight there's a sick mum who can't look after her two young children aged two and four. Good heavens, why is thatstupid woman flying, if she's ill? And why hasn't she got something for her kids with her? There are books, gameboys, there's music to listen to and films to watch on a 13-hour-flight. And what do they expect me to do with the kids? Play games with them? Show them around the plane? There's nothing much to see on a plane, is there?

1. *name:* Lisa Hopkins
*age:* 17
*marital status:* single
*children:* –
*education:* languages good; science bad
*suitable/not suitable/because ...:* general standard of education is not good enough (not interested in politics, science, sport); does not keep to safety rules

*name:* Helen Baxter
*age:* 21
*marital status:* single
*children:* –
*education:* low general knowledge
*suitable/not suitable/because ...:* does not react the right way (leaves passenger in a burning car); no courage (fighting youngsters); not a diplomat; lack of energy (she needs her sleep)

*name:* Neil Jenkins
*age:* 28
*marital status:* married
*children:* 1 (baby son)
*education:* at university; is studying law; high standard of education
*suitable/not suitable/because ...:* wants the job because of the free flights; no feeling for people (sick woman); does not want to look after children (cannot or doesn't want to entertain them)

2. 1. That was Helen.
2. That was Neil.
3. That was Lisa.
4. That was Helen.
5. That was Lisa.
6. That was Helen.

3. **Lösungsvorschlag:**
Lisa should prepare herself more carefully. She has to entertain passengers and she could meet someone who is interested in technical details of the plane. She must be able to answer those questions. She should start reading newspapers, because it might be important to advise passengers about what to read and to tell the difference between newspapers. She must know what to hand out if a person wants to be informed or just entertained during the flight. Sometimes she has to start a conversation and if she finds out that a passenger is interested in sports or politics, she will have to be able to continue a conversation. At least she should ask questions to show her interest, but without knowing anything about the subject you can't even do that.
Helen's problem is quite different. She lacks all sorts of basic essentials: she doesn't show any initiative, she has not enough energy to last a 13-hour-flight, she doesn't feel responsible for her passengers. She has no idea what to do and how to react in dangerous situations. Of course, you have to save the passengers if the plane is on fire or if people start a fight you have to be able to calm them down. Her idea of calling the police is ridiculous (you don't usually have the police on a plane).
Neil made a lot of mistakes, too. Although he has got a baby son he cannot imagine that children want to be occupied during a boring flight. He doesn't show any sympathy either for the sick woman or for her children who might be upset about their sick mother.
Neil pointed out why he wanted the job. His main reason was that he wanted free flights for himself and his family. The next time he applies for such a job he should not talk about this aspect so openly. He also mentioned that he didn't want the job for life. A company cannot be interested in someone who gets the training and then leaves the job. I don't think Neil should apply for this kind of job at all, because he would be away from his family most of the time and he wouldn't like that.

## 4 The mobile office

1. 1. paragraph 5; 2 paragraph 2; 3. paragraph 1; 4. paragraph 6; 5. paragraph 3; 6 paragraph 4

2. a) *Denkbar:*
– office buildings are no longer necessary
– money and time are saved because expensive rooms for working are no longer needed
– you can keep in touch with staff all the time because they are fully networked